Sport psychology

Sport Psychology provides an introductory account of the major psychological issues in sport today. Major theories and up-to-date research are covered in the areas of personality, attitudes to sport, aggression in sport, anxiety and stress, social influences, motivation and skill acquisition. A wide variety of sporting examples support the text, ranging from football to ballet.

This highly readable and detailed account of sport psychology will interest introductory students in sports psychology and sports studies, whether at college or university, as well as the general reader.

Matt Jarvis is Senior Teaching Psychologist at Totton College and Totton Sports Academy.

Routledge Modular Psychology

Series editors: Cara Flanagan is a Reviser for AS and A2 level Psychology and is an experienced author and teacher. Philip Banyard is Associate Senior Lecturer in Psychology at Nottingham Trent University and a Chief Examiner for AS and A2 level Psychology. Both are experienced writers.

The *Routledge Modular Psychology* series is a completely new approach to introductory-level psychology, tailor-made to the new modular style of teaching. Each short book covers a topic in more detail than any large textbook can, allowing teacher and student to select material exactly to suit any particular course or project.

The books have been written especially for those students new to higher-level study, whether at school, college or university. They include specially designed features to help with technique, such as a model essay at an average level with an examiner's comments to show how extra marks can be gained. The authors are all examiners and teachers at the introductory level.

The *Routledge Modular Psychology* texts are all user-friendly and accessible and include the following features:

- practice essays with specialist commentary to show how to achieve a higher grade
- chapter summaries to assist with revision
- progress and review exercises
- glossary of key terms
- summaries of key research
- further reading to stimulate ongoing study and research
- cross-referencing to other books in the series

Also available in this series (titles listed by syllabus section):

Sport psychology

Matt Jarvis

ROUTLEDGE
ROUTLEDGE
Taylor & Francis Group

First published 1999
by Routledge
11 New Fetter Lane, London EC4P 4EE

Reprinted 2000

Reprinted 2002
by Routledge
27 Church Road, Hove, East Sussex BN3 2FA

Simultaneously published in the USA and Canada
by Routledge
29 West 35th Street, New York, NY 10001

Routledge is an imprint of the Taylor & Francis Group

© 1999 Matt Jarvis

Typeset in Frutiger and Times by Routledge
Printed and bound in Great Britain by
St Edmundsbury Press, Bury St Edmunds, Suffolk

British Library Cataloguing in Publication Data
A catalogue record for this book is available from the British Library

Library of Congress Cataloging in Publication Data
Jarvis, Matt, 1966–
Sport psychology / Matt Jarvis.
(Routledge Modular Psychology)
Includes bibliographical references and index.
1. Sports – psychological aspects. 2. Athletes – psychology.
I. Title. II. Series.
GV706.4.J37   1999   99-12984
796'.01–dc21   CIP

ISBN 0–415–20641–3 (hbk)
ISBN 0–415–20642–1 (pbk)

Contents

Illustrations

Figures

Tables

Acknowledgements

This book would not have been possible without the support of numerous colleagues, friends and family. I would particularly like to thank psychologists Peter Terry, Rob Lewis and Anthony Curtis for their technical advice, and sporting gurus Phil and Clare Sinkinson, Kev Cleary, John McClearie and Tony Meenaghan for contributing their sporting knowledge. Cara Flanagan, Moira Taylor, Viv Ward and Alison Dixon at Routledge have my gratitude for their kind and expert support at all stages of the project. My colleagues Julia Russell and Craig Roberts, like my long-suffering students at Totton College, have been consistently encouraging and offered valuable advice. Most of all, I would like to thank Clare, who has spent many evenings abandoned while I was hunched over the computer.

The series editors and Routledge acknowledge the OCR (Oxford, Cambridge and RSA Examinations) for permission to reproduce the exam questions in the Study Aids chapter of the book. This body bears no responsibility for the example answers to questions taken from its past examination papers which are contained in this publication.

Introduction to sport psychology

 What is sport psychology?
A brief history of sport psychology
What is a sport psychologist?

What is sport psychology?

Because there are many ways in which we can apply psychology to sport and given the wide range of activities that different cultures regard as sport, we need to adopt quite a broad definition of sport psychology. In 1996 the European Federation of Sport Psychology (FEPSAC) produced such a broad definition which, slightly simplified, reads: *Sport psychology is the study of the psychological basis, processes and effects of sport.* The term 'sport' is used, both in the FEPSAC definition of sport psychology and throughout this book, in the broad sense, including any physical activity for the purposes of competition, recreation, education or health. Psychology can be defined as 'the science of mind and behaviour' (Gross 1996).

Sport psychology, then, is a broad field. American sport psychologists draw a sharp distinction between **academic sport psychology**, which focuses on all the factors affecting participation and performance in sport, and **applied sport psychology**, which focuses purely on applying psychology to enhance athletic performance (e.g. Cox 1998). So far, European writers have not usually made this distinction (Kremer and Scully 1994) and this book crosses freely between academic and applied sport psychology. The topics covered here, personality, attitudes, aggression, stress and anxiety, group dynamics, motivation and skill acquisition should be both of academic interest, and applicable to working with athletes and in some cases spectators.

A brief history of sport psychology

Sport psychology has existed in some form for almost as long as psychology itself. The first recorded study in sport psychology took place at the close of the nineteenth century. Norman Triplett (1898) performed what is often cited as the first experiment in social psychology as well as the first in sport psychology. Triplett invest-igated the phenomenon of social facilitation (discussed in detail in Chapter 6). He demonstrated that cyclists tended to cycle faster when racing against another cyclist than they could alone. Triplett did not pursue further sport-related research however and it was not until the 1920s that the discipline of sport psychology was formally estab-lished.

In 1925, Coleman Griffith set up the Athletic Research Laboratory at the University of Illinois. Griffith, who also put sport psychology on the map by establishing a university course, publishing two major textbooks and acting as consultant to professional sports teams, is often called the 'father of sport psychology'. The early path of sport psychology did not run smoothly however, and the Athletic Research Laboratory closed in 1932 due to lack of funds.

Between the 1930s and the 1960s (at least in the Western world) there was little activity in the field of sport psychology. In the Soviet Union, sport psychology emerged as a discipline shortly after the Second World War. It is of course difficult to obtain accurate infor-mation about the practice of Soviet psychology during the Cold War, but it is commonly believed that, during the 1960 Melbourne Olympics, Eastern European teams employed sport psychologists (Kremer and Scully 1994). Certainly we know that, by the early 1970s, East German and Russian teams were routinely employing sport psychologists to enhance athletic performance in international events.

Sport psychology reappeared in the USA in the 1960s, and was taken up in Britain and the rest of Europe a few years later. The area has since expanded worldwide to become one of the fastest growing new academic disciplines. Interestingly, until very recently the study of sport psychology was firmly located in the domain of sport sciences as opposed to within psychology. This may be changing however: in 1986 the American Psychological Association officially recognised sport psychology as a branch of psychology and in 1993 the British Psychological Society formed a Sport and Exercise Psychology Section.

What is a sport psychologist?

This question can be thought of in two ways: who can call themselves a sport psychologist, and what do sport psychologists do? To address the first question, currently in Britain there is no compulsory registration of sport psychologists, therefore (in theory) anyone can call themselves a sport psychologist. In reality of course, it would be highly unethical for anyone not properly trained to use the title 'psychologist' in any context. The British Association of Sport and Exercise Sciences (BASES) keeps a register of approved sport psychologists. At the 1998 annual conference, the British Psychological Society's Sport and Exercise Psychology Section approved the principle of granting the title 'Chartered Sport Psychologist' to appropriately qualified people. To register with BASES as a sport psychologist you need either a first degree in psychology and a higher degree in sport science or a first degree in sport science and a higher degree in sport psychology. To achieve chartered status from the British Psychological Society, it is necessary to have a BPS-approved first degree in psychology and a BPS-approved postgraduate training, including supervised practice.

There is some controversy surrounding the accreditation of sport psychologists. The BASES scheme for registration of sport psychologists has only existed since 1992 and many people who were already working as sport psychologists chose not to join the register or were unqualified to do so. Anshell (1992) has pointed out that many of those working full-time with athletes do not have the time, resources or inclination to pursue the lengthy procedures necessary to become registered, and that registration thus excludes some of Britain's most experienced practitioners. On the other hand, compulsory registration would provide a measure of protection for the public from dubious or underqualified practitioners. The issue of accreditation is likely to come to a head if the use of the term 'psychologist' becomes legally restricted, as is already true in some countries and is likely to become the case in Britain in the next century.

With regard to the second question, the work sport psychologists do is quite varied. The European Federation of Sport Psychology (1996) recognise three inter-related tasks for sport psychologists:

- *research*: investigation into all aspects of the psychology of sport, both theoretical and applied.
- *education*: teaching students, officials and athletes about sport psychology.
- *application*: assessment of, and intervention in, psychological problems connected to sport. This can involve acting as consultant to whole teams or counselling individuals.

Because sport psychology is now such a broad field, it is becoming impossible for sport psychologists to keep up with all aspects of their discipline. Nowadays, you will find that many sport psychologists have become highly specialised. For example, a psychologist may specialise in the area of motivation (see Chapter 7). They may carry out research into motivation, teach coaches about motivation and perhaps work with individual athletes to improve their motivation.

Further reading

European Federation of Sport Psychology (1996) Position statement of the FEPSAC: 1. Definition of sport psychology. *The sport psychologist* 10, 221–3. A brief official document explaining the aims and scope of sport psychology and its relationship to other disciplines.

Kremer J and Scully D (1994) *Psychology in sport*. London, Taylor & Francis. An excellent general account of the development of sport psychology, particularly interesting in its coverage of the relationship between sport and academic psychology and its analysis of the accreditation issue.

Williams JM (ed.) (1993) *Applied sport psychology, personal growth to peak performance*, Mountain View, Mayfield. A clear and detailed account of the history of sport psychology, covering America and Eastern Europe.

2

Personality and sport

Introduction

One of the most basic questions faced by psychology is 'why are we all different?' Of course in some ways we are all much the same, for example in the structure of our brains and the mechanisms of perception and memory. However there are huge differences between us in the ways we think, feel and behave in different situations. The psychology of personality is concerned with these individual differences. Pervin (1993) offered a simple working definition of personality: *Personality represents those characteristics of the person that account for consistent patterns of behaviour*. Broadly, four factors influence how we respond in any given situation: our genetic make-up, our past experience, the nature of the situation in which we find ourselves and our free will. Each of these factors is emphasised by one or more theories of personality.

Trait theories of personality emphasise the role of genetics in determining our individuality. **Social learning theory**, by contrast, sees personality as primarily determined by past experience. Situational and interactional views place more emphasis on the particular situation and less emphasis on the nature of the individual in determining how they act. Trait, social learning, situational and interactional theories are all ambitious approaches to personality that aim to describe the entire nature of the person. **Narrow-band theories** are less ambitious, focusing on a single aspect of personality. None of the main theoretical approaches to personality place much emphasis on free will, i.e. how we choose to think, feel and behave. Free will is a controversial idea in psychology. Although we may believe that we choose how to behave, it is always likely that we are influenced to some degree by our genetic make-up and our past experiences.

The study of personality can be said to underlie all sport psychology. When we look in later chapters at such topics as attitudes, aggression, motivation and anxiety, what we are really interested in is how and why people differ in these aspects, and how we can modify these to improve athletic performance. The answers to many of these questions can be found in personality theory.

Trait theories

There are two main assumptions underlying the trait approach to personality. First, an individual's personality is made up of certain key characteristics or *traits*. Traits are the stable, enduring characteristics of a person. Second, individuals differ in each trait due to genetic differences. Traits can be measured according to three factors: their frequency, their intensity and the range of situations to which they can be applied. For example, a trait that appears in most of the major theories is extroversion – how lively, sociable and impulsive an individual is. We know someone is very extrovert if they display this kind of behaviour often, to an extreme and in a variety of quite different situations.

Eysenck's theory

Eysenck (1952) initially proposed that personality could be completely described by just two traits: extroversion and neuroticism. Extroversion describes how lively, sociable and impulsive a person is, while neuroticism describes how emotionally stable they are. One question you might ask is why three different characteristics like liveliness, sociability and impulsivity are grouped together as one trait. The answer is that, through a mathematical process called **factor analysis**, Eysenck discovered that in most cases it is the *same people* who tend to be lively, impulsive and sociable. When characteristic behaviours tend to go together in this way, we can say that they make up one trait. Extroversion and neuroticism can be measured by a personality test called the Eysenck Personality Inventory (EPI). Some items from the EPI are shown in Table 2.1.

Table 2.1 Items from the Eysenck Personality Inventory	Yes	No
1 Do you often long for excitement?	❏	❏
2 Do you often need understanding friends to cheer you up?	❏	❏
3 Are you usually carefree?	❏	❏
4 Do you find it very hard to take no for an answer?	❏	❏
5 Do you stop and think things over before doing anything?	❏	❏

You can probably see that Questions 1, 3 and 5 are part of the extroversion (E) scale, while Questions 2 and 4 are part of the neuroticism (N) scale. The E and N scales are each marked out of 24. A high score on the E scale would indicate that you are very extrovert while a low score would indicate that you are very introvert, i.e. quiet, solitary and not at all impulsive.

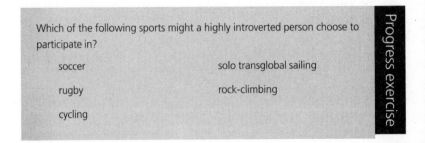

Which of the following sports might a highly introverted person choose to participate in?

soccer   solo transglobal sailing

rugby   rock-climbing

cycling

Progress exercise

A high score on the N scale would indicate that you are very neurotic, i.e. emotionally unstable, whereas a very low score would indicate that you are a very stable, 'unflappable' person. This is shown in Figure 2.1.

	EPI score	
introvert	1 2 3 4 5 6 7 8 9 10 11 12 *E scale* 13 14 15 16 17 18 19 20 21 22 23 24	extrovert
stable	1 2 3 4 5 6 7 8 9 10 11 12 *N scale* 13 14 15 16 17 18 19 20 21 22 23 24	neurotic

Figure 2.1 **What Eysenck Personality Inventory scores show**

Most people score between 5 and 20 on each scale. In a later version of his theory, Eysenck (1975) added a third personality trait – psychoticism – a measure of how tender or tough-minded an individual is. This factor is incorporated into a third scale in Eysenck's later personality test, the Eysenck Personality Questionnaire (EPQ).

Eysenck (1966) explained extroversion and neuroticism as being primarily determined by the nature of the individual's nervous system. Introverts are more easily aroused by events than extroverts, therefore they require less stimulation to be comfortable. Introverts tend to seek out situations where there is relatively little stimulation, appearing quiet and solitary. Extroverts, who require more stimulation to achieve a comfortable level of arousal, respond by seeking out situations where there is more stimulation to be had. Their behaviour therefore tends to be more lively and sociable.

Eysenck saw neuroticism as being a result of the response of the individual's nervous system to stress. Those who score highly in neuroticism are thus those whose nervous system responds strongly to stress and is slow to recover. Stable people would be those whose nervous system responded less strongly to stress and then recovered more quickly.

Paul Gascoigne and Jimmy White are two sportsmen known and well-liked for their personalities. However, despite their acknowledged brilliance, Paul Gascoigne was dropped from the 1998 English World Cup squad and Jimmy White never won the snooker world championship. Referring to Eysenck's theory:

1 What personality factors might have contributed to Paul Gascoigne's and Jimmy White's popularity?
2 What personality factors might have limited their achievements?

Cattell's theory

Cattell (1965) disagreed with Eysenck's view that personality could be understood by looking at only three dimensions of behaviour. Instead he argued that it was necessary to look at a much larger number of traits in order to get a complete picture of someone's personality. Like Eysenck, Cattell used the mathematical technique of factor analysis to look at which types of behaviour tended to be grouped together in the same people. He identified sixteen personality factors. Cattell's sixteen personality traits are shown in Figure 2.2.

Cattell produced a personality test similar to the EPI that measured each of the sixteen traits. The 16PF (as it is called) has 160 questions in total, 10 questions relating to each personality factor.

Eysenck proposed that Cattell's sixteen factors would fit neatly within his three. For example, the relaxed–tense factor, the placid–apprehensive factor and the stable–unstable factor are all subsumed by Eysenck's trait of neuroticism. The argument between Eysenck and Cattell is really a mathematical one. To sport psychologists what matters is not who got their sums right but which test is

Figure 2.2 Cattell's sixteen personality factors

more useful in understanding sporting performance. Studies using Eysenck's and Cattell's theories and personality tests in relation to sport will be reviewed later in this chapter.

Other measurable personality variables

Trait theories-proper aim to explain *all* individual variation in personality. A number of more modest theories have looked at specific aspects of personality. We call these narrow-band theories. Many of these will come up again in the next few chapters as they relate to such factors as competitive anxiety, achievement-motivation, etc. However, research relating to narrow-band theories will be included in the following discussion of the relationship between personality and sport. Two narrow-band approaches to personality are worth a particularly close look: **sensation seeking** and **telic dominance**.

Sensation seeking

Zuckerman (1979) identified sensation seeking as an aspect of personality. Sensation seeking reflects the amount of stimulation a person will seek. Zuckerman identified four separate factors that make up sensation seeking. These are: seeking of thrills and adventure, tendency to act on impulse, seeking of new experiences and vulnerability to boredom. Zuckerman has produced a personality test measuring sensation seeking. Some items from Zuckerman's scale are shown in Table 2.2.

Studies have found that sensation seeking, as measured by Zuckerman's scale, is positively related to drug-taking, sexual experimentation, public drunkenness and volunteering for high-risk activities. Clearly, the latter is of interest to sport psychologists, who are interested in who chooses to participate in risky sports.

Telic dominance

The idea of telic dominance comes from the wider field of reversal theory, an approach to explaining human motivation. According to reversal theory, we all alternate between telic states in which we avoid arousal and **paratelic states** in which we seek arousal. Some of us are said to be dominated by telic states and others by paratelic states, i.e.

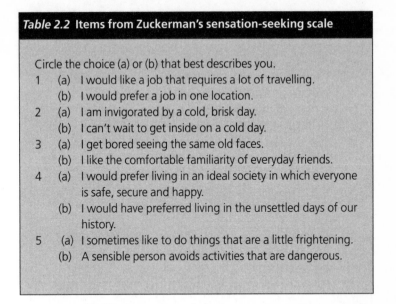

Table 2.2 Items from Zuckerman's sensation-seeking scale

Circle the choice (a) or (b) that best describes you.

1   (a)   I would like a job that requires a lot of travelling.
    (b)   I would prefer a job in one location.
2   (a)   I am invigorated by a cold, brisk day.
    (b)   I can't wait to get inside on a cold day.
3   (a)   I get bored seeing the same old faces.
    (b)   I like the comfortable familiarity of everyday friends.
4   (a)   I would prefer living in an ideal society in which everyone is safe, secure and happy.
    (b)   I would have preferred living in the unsettled days of our history.
5   (a)   I sometimes like to do things that are a little frightening.
    (b)   A sensible person avoids activities that are dangerous.

we spend most of our time in one or the other state. We are thus said to be telic dominant or paratelic dominant. Murgatroyd *et al.* (1978) have produced a personality test designed to measure telic dominance. Some items from Murgatroyd's Telic Dominance Scale (TDS) are shown in Table 2.3.

Kerr (1997) proposed that telic-dominant and paratelic-dominant individuals will react differently to stress. They may also have different preferences in their choice of sport.

Applying trait and narrow-band theories to sport

Of all the approaches to personality, most research in sport psychology has involved the trait and narrow-band approaches. Attempts have been made to distinguish athletes from non-athletes and successful performers from less successful performers. Sport psychologists have also looked at whether personality factors are associated with choice of sport.

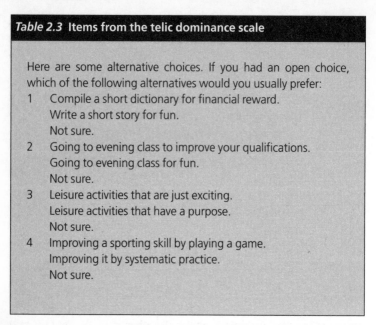

Table 2.3 Items from the telic dominance scale

Here are some alternative choices. If you had an open choice, which of the following alternatives would you usually prefer:

1 Compile a short dictionary for financial reward.
   Write a short story for fun.
   Not sure.
2 Going to evening class to improve your qualifications.
   Going to evening class for fun.
   Not sure.
3 Leisure activities that are just exciting.
   Leisure activities that have a purpose.
   Not sure.
4 Improving a sporting skill by playing a game.
   Improving it by systematic practice.
   Not sure.

Progress exercise

Make a list of the athletes and non-athletes among your friends. Using the theories discussed so far, can you think of anything the athletes generally have in common, that distinguishes them from the non-athletes?

Distinguishing athletes from non-athletes

Numerous attempts have been made to find out whether there is a fundamental difference in the personality of athletes and non-athletes. Eysenck *et al.* (1982) proposed that people scoring high on the extroversion and psychoticism scales of the EPQ are more likely to take up sport. This has not however been supported by research (Kremer and Scully 1994). Schurr *et al.* (1977) tested 1,500 American students with the 16PF, relating this to participation in sport, choice of sport and level of success. They found that athletes differed from non-athletes on three scales of the 16PF, being more independent and objective, and less anxious than the non-athletes. Overall, the research is equivocal and different writers have reached different conclusions about whether athletes and non-athletes have different personalities.

Distinguishing successful from unsuccessful athletes

An early attempt to use the idea of personality traits to identify successful athletes was by Tutko and Ogilvie (1966). They proposed that successful people score highly on eleven personality traits: aggression, coachability, conscientiousness, determination, drive, emotional control, guilt-proneness, leadership, mental toughness, self-confidence and trust. Tutko and Ogilvie produced a personality test called the Athletic Motivation Inventory (AMI) which aimed to measure these traits. Most sport psychologists agree that the AMI was seriously flawed and contemporary research does not support the idea that the AMI can distinguish between successful and unsuccessful athletes.

Studies using superior personality tests have found some evidence that aspects of personality are associated with athletic success. Garland and Barry (1990) placed American college athletes in categories representing their level of skill. They were then tested with the 16PF. The statistical relationship between their athletic success and the personality factors measured by the 16PF was calculated. It emerged that tough-mindedness, extroversion, group dependence and emotional stability accounted for 29 per cent of the variance in skill. This shows that although personality may have been one important factor in success, there were other probably more important factors.

In another study, Lerner and Locke (1995) measured the competitiveness and achievement-motivation of sixty male American undergraduates, using a personality test called the Sport Orientation Questionnaire (SOQ). They then subjected them to an endurance task involving sit-ups. A positive relationship between personality and success of similar strength to that in the Garland and Barry study was found. However, it was found that other psychological factors such as goal-setting and self-efficacy (see Chapter 7) could override the effect of personality.

Although these results show that we have had moderate success in relating personality characteristics to success in sport, there are some important provisos to bear in mind. First, not all studies have confirmed this type of relationship. For example, Davis (1991) attempted to predict success in the selection of professional ice-hockey players in trials by measuring personality traits and found no relationship between selection and personality. Second, there are serious limits to the usefulness of knowing that there is some relationship between personality and success. Although we can help improve an individual's motivation and focus, and we can help athletes manage their anxiety, we cannot fundamentally change someone's personality. Neither, as Davis demonstrated, can we select people purely on the basis of their personality, when there are more important factors, both psychological and physical, affecting performance.

Personality and choice of sport

This has proved a rather more fruitful area of study and some important differences between the personalities of successful athletes in different sports have emerged. This is hardly surprising when you consider the different demands of different sports. In the Schurr *et al.* (1977) study, although relatively few differences emerged between athletes and non-athletes, considerable differences were found between team and individual players. Team players emerged as more anxious and extrovert than individual competitors. Clingman and Hilliard (1987) found that super-adherers – i.e. those who excelled at endurance sports such as triathlon – were unusually high in achievement-motivation, autonomy, dominance and harm-avoidance. McGill *et al.* (1986) looked at rock-climbers and found that they were particularly high on sensation seeking and low on anxiety.

Telic dominance has been used to successfully distinguish between participants in different sports. In one Spanish study, Chirivella and Martinez (1994) compared tennis players (low risk), karateka (medium risk) and parasailors (high risk) on the telic dominance scale. Significant differences emerged, particularly on the anxiety-avoidance subscale, where parasailors scored considerably lower than the other groups.

Figure 2.3 **Climbers are often high in sensation seeking and low in anxiety**

Source: Reproduced by kind permission of Julia Russell

Evaluation of the trait and narrow-band approaches

The usefulness of the trait approach largely depends on its success in measuring personality. Personality tests derived from trait theories, such as the EPI and 16PF, are called **self-rating inventories**. There are numerous problems with this type of test and, if you have ever filled in an EPI and received a score, you would be well-advised not to take the results too seriously. The EPI has limited test–retest reliability, i.e. if you test someone and then test them again a few days or weeks later they will only tend to give the same responses to about 80 per cent of the questions. Answers to this type of test are influenced by mood and the social desirability of the answers – most people would rather be seen as extrovert than introvert and as stable rather than neurotic. Who administers the test and how they do so (e.g. alone or in a group) can also affect people's responses.

Ultimately, the trait approach to personality has yielded some fascinating results, but has limited application in sport psychology. As already discussed, we cannot radically change someone's personality traits in order to make them a better athlete. Nor would it be wise to use personality traits as a way of selecting athletes – seeing people perform will always be a better test of their potential. One way in which the trait approach can be useful, however, is in profiling individual athletes so that the sport psychologist can identify the type of difficulties that individual is likely to encounter. **Personality profiling** involves measuring an athlete on a number of personality scales and building up a picture of their strengths and weaknesses. We might, for example, find that when a promising athlete is profiled, their only weakness is in achievement-motivation or competitive anxiety. A coach can benefit from knowing this and may choose to manage that athlete accordingly. However, the best profiles of this type do not just measure personality traits but other psychological factors as well. We shall return to the issue of profiling when discussing the interactional approach.

Situational and interactional approaches

One of the problems with trait theories, and to some extent with narrow-band theories as well, is that they assume the individual's behaviour is consistent across a variety of situations. This largely ignores the impact that the situation itself has on the person's response. Mischel (1968) put forward the situationalist approach. This was a radical theory that rejected entirely the idea of stable personality traits. Instead, Mischel proposed that people's responses to situations could be explained entirely by the specifics of the situation. Effectively, this is a rejection of the whole concept of personality.

Progress exercise

Imagine you are about to compete in a practice sprint at your local college or club. There are a few friends around, but no one is paying you too much attention. No other serious runners are taking part. Now imagine instead that you are lining up for the final of the Olympic 100 metres.

1 List all the aspects of these two situations you can think of that differ.
2 How might your response to these two situations differ?

Nowadays virtually no psychologists would accept situationalism as a complete explanation of behaviour. Mischel (1990) has himself back-tracked somewhat, while still maintaining the important point that the way individuals think, feel and act in different situations varies considerably more than we would expect if trait theory were entirely correct. The idea that our behaviour at any time is a product of an interaction between the situation and our personality is called the interactional view, first proposed by Bowers (1973).

Applying the interactional model to sport

The vignette in the progress exercise above should illustrate the importance of situations. However, we can understand people's behaviour better if we look at how the situation interacts with their personality. You probably know someone who is a friendly, jolly character who, in their social life, would not hurt a fly, yet on the sportsfield seems almost uncontrollably aggressive. We cannot explain this person's actions by situation or personality alone. We know that they are not simply an aggressive person because their behaviour is not aggressive in other situations. We also know that competing on the sportsfield does not make the rest of us uncontrollably aggressive. Therefore, this individual's aggression when taking part in sport must result from some complex interaction between their personality and the sporting situation.

Cox (1998) has estimated the importance of various factors in sporting performance. Personality, situation and the interaction between personality and situation together account for less than half the variance in athletic performance. This is shown in Figure 2.4.

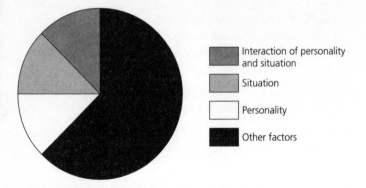

Figure 2.4 **The relative importance of personality, situation and other factors in athletic performance**

Source: Cox (1998)

Profiling moods

We know that although we can produce profiles of athletes' personalities, this is not particularly useful in predicting how well they will perform. However, the interactional model gives us another angle on profiling. Instead of trying to measure people's underlying personality traits, we can instead measure their *mood* at the time of performance. An athlete's mood at any one time is a product of both personality *and* situation, therefore it is a much more valid measure of their psychological state during performance. McNair *et al.* (1972) developed the Profile Of Mood States (POMS), a sixty-five-item questionnaire that assesses individuals on six scales: tension, depression, anger, vigour, fatigue and confusion. POMS was originally developed for assessing the state of psychiatric patients, but it quickly caught on in the field of sport psychology.

Morgan (1979) has produced the mood profile for elite athletes, by measuring them on each of the POMS scales. Figure 2.5 shows the classic iceberg profile of an elite athlete. The flatter profile of the less successful athlete is also shown. Elite athletes score lower on most mood measures, notably on tension and depression, but higher on vigour. Numerous studies have shown that elite athletes from a variety of sports do in fact tend to exhibit the iceberg profile. Thus Bell and Howe (1988) found iceberg profiles in triathletes, and Morgan *et al.*

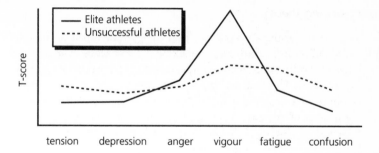

Figure 2.5 **Mood profiles of elite and unsuccessful athletes**

Source: Morgan (1979)

(1987, 1988) found the same pattern in long-distance runners. Asken (1991) found that elite disabled athletes similarly exhibited the iceberg profile.

Evaluation of the interactional approach

As the interactional approach looks at how individuals respond to specific sport-related situations, it is more useful than the trait approach for predicting athletic performance. Of course, in practice the two approaches can be used together. When profiles of individual athletes are drawn up for training purposes, the best profiles include information about both personality and mood states.

In her review of personality research in sport, Vealey (1989) identifies a shift away from trait measurement since the 1970s in favour of the interactional approach. However, this approach is not without its critics. Some sport psychologists reject the idea of testing athletes for mood or traits. Prapavessis and Grove (1991) point out that where studies compare average POMS scores of elite and unsuccessful athletes, these averages obscure wide individual differences. Thus there are highly successful performers who do not exhibit an iceberg profile. In general, POMS scores are only moderately predictive of performance.

Social learning theory

The social learning approach to psychology (developed in Bandura 1977) differs from trait and interactional approaches in that it sees individual differences in behaviour as resulting from different *learning experiences*. This means that what determines an individual's response to a situation is not so much their genetic make-up or the constraints of the particular situation, but instead how past experience has taught that person to act. Because of the emphasis on learned behaviour, social learning theory falls under the broader umbrella of **behavioural psychology**. Although social learning theory is not the only psychological approach that emphasises the role of past experience on personality, it is the most influential such theory in sport psychology.

Bandura (1977) proposed that learning of behaviour takes place in two main ways: **operant conditioning** and modelling. Operant conditioning involves learning by reinforcement. When we experiment with a new behaviour there are four possible outcomes: positive reinforcement, negative reinforcement, a neutral response and punishment. Positive reinforcement involves the behaviour being *rewarded*. Negative reinforcement involves *failing to be punished* for the behaviour. A neutral response means that *no positive or negative consequences* result from the behaviour. Punishment involves introducing *an unpleasant consequence*. Clearly if we try out a behaviour and something positive results, we are rewarded. The behaviour is thus said to be positively reinforced, and we learn that it is a 'good' or 'useful' behaviour and add it to our repertoire of behaviours. Similarly, if we commit a suspect behaviour and escape punishment we are negatively reinforced, and are likely to repeat the behaviour. If, on the other hand, the behaviour does not achieve anything (neutral response), or if it results in something nasty happening to us (punishment), we are not likely to repeat it.

Modelling involves learning new behaviours by watching and copying the behaviour of others. Bandura has proposed that learning of behaviour takes place in four stages:

- *attention*: we watch others behave in a certain way
- *retention*: we commit what we have watched to memory
- *reproduction*: we try out the behaviour ourselves

- *reinforcement*: we consider the consequences of the behaviour and decide whether or not to repeat it.

We do not have to experience reinforcement personally to learn from it. If we observe someone else's behaviour being rewarded we can add that behaviour to our own repertoire. This is called **vicarious reinforcement**. We can similarly learn by seeing someone punished *or escaping punishment* following a behaviour.

Applying social learning theory to sport

Social learning theory will crop up throughout this book. It provides at least a partial explanation of individual differences in attitudes, aggression and motivation. Two applications of social learning are particularly worth considering in this chapter, explaining how we acquire patterns of sport-related behaviour and explaining how we acquire a love of sport.

Patterns of sport-related behaviour

To social learning psychologists, personality is not something we are born with but simply a set of learned behaviour patterns. Some of these learned patterns of behaviour can be quite specific to sport. Earlier in the chapter we considered how we might explain why some people display very aggressive behaviour during sport, even though they do not appear aggressive in other situations. Social learning theory would explain this in terms of the individual learning that aggression is the correct response to the sporting situation. This might mean that somehow they had received reinforcement for acting aggressively in the past, e.g. scoring a point or receiving a pat on the back or a 'that's my boy' from a coach or parent following an aggressive act. Using Bandura's model, this might be represented by the following sequence:

- *attention*: a child witnesses a very aggressive tackle while watching football on television
- *retention*: the knowledge of aggressive tackling is retained in memory

- *reproduction*: next time the child is playing football, they copy the technique of aggressive tackling
- *reinforcement*: if the aggressive tackle receives reinforcement (e.g. it prevents a goal, receives praise etc.), it is likely to become the child's regular behaviour.

It might alternatively be that the person had witnessed a sportsperson acting aggressively during a game and seen them profit from the aggression. This would be an example of vicarious reinforcement.

Athletes as role models

An important implication of the fact that children tend to copy the sport-related behaviour of adults is that any athlete in the public eye provides a **role model** for children. Given that the huge majority of sportspeople conduct themselves admirably and regularly demonstrate to young people the importance of hard work, perseverance, cooperation and a 'sporting' attitude, the world of sport can give itself a collective pat on the back and acknowledge that they probably contribute very significantly to the healthy development of young people. Some sportspeople, such as Jonathan Edwards and Kris Akabusi, provide particularly good role models by visiting local schools and conducting training sessions. The other side of the coin is that, from a social learning viewpoint, it is important that poor behaviour by high-profile athletes is punished. If public figures in sport are seen to behave inappropriately and profit from doing so, children may receive vicarious reinforcement and copy the inappropriate behaviour.

Acquiring love of sport

One very obvious question that sport psychologists have probably not asked enough is 'why are we so obsessed with sport in the first place?' From a trait perspective, Eysenck et al. (1982) proposed that people of a certain personality type were naturally attracted to sport. However, social learning theory can provide perhaps a better explanation, although it may not be in itself a complete answer. Children (perhaps, especially boys) receive positive reinforcement from a very young age if they show interest in and talent for sport. We also receive vicarious reinforcement every time we see an athlete win and enjoy the benefits of winning. As parents and coaches, it is important to remember that if we want young people to acquire a love of sport we should provide them with plenty of positive experiences of sport. If, as has been sadly common in the past, teachers only provide positive reinforcers for the talented few, we should not be surprised when those children who have been ignored do not develop what we might consider a healthy love of sport.

Evaluation of social learning theory

There is little doubt that, even if our personality is to some extent influenced by genetics as the trait theorists believe, our patterns of behaviour are also strongly influenced by childhood learning experiences. From the perspective of a sport psychologist there is one huge advantage of social learning theory. Unlike trait and interactional approaches, social learning theory sees the personality of the athlete as *modifiable*. This means that we can intervene and shape athletes' sporting behaviour patterns. We can also use sport as a general socialising agent to aid healthy psychological development in children.

Summary

Personality theories aim to explain why we, as individuals, behave as we do in different situations. Trait theories, such as those of Eysenck and Cattell, suggest that the main influences on our behaviour are biological and governed by genetics. Personality traits have found few differences between athletes and non-athletes, but some traits seem to be associated with sporting success and the choice of certain sports. Interactional theories propose that our behaviour is a product of an interplay between genetic differences and the characteristics of the current situation. This approach has proved particularly useful in sport psychology, allowing personality profiles of successful athletes to be constructed. Social learning theory emphasises the role of learning behaviour from others, particularly in childhood. It has helped us to understand how children learn sport-related behaviour and attitudes towards sport (explored further in Chapter 3).

Review exercise

Choose a well-known figure from your own main sport. Write down everything you know about their behaviour during matches and their general behaviour off the sportsfield.

1 How would trait theory explain what you know about them?
2 How would interactional theory explain what you know about them?
3 How would social learning theory explain what you know about them?

Further reading

Cox R (1998) *Sport psychology, concepts and applications*. Boston, McGraw-Hill. Perhaps the most comprehensive review of research in the area of personality and sport. Good coverage of methods of personality measurement. Particularly balanced coverage of male and female athletes, and able-bodied and disabled athletes.

Gill DL (1986) *Psychological dynamics of sport*. Champaign, Human Kinetics. Particularly useful coverage of personality profiling in sport and the issue of personality screening of athletes.

Pervin L (1993) *Personality theory and research*. New York, Wiley. Not focused on sport, but an excellent general text, covering all the major theoretical approaches to personality. Good coverage of different ways of measuring personality and good evaluations of trait and social learning theories.

3

Attitudes to sport

The nature of attitudes
Measuring attitudes
The formation of attitudes to sport
Attitudes to sport and sporting behaviour
Changing people's attitudes to sport
Summary

Aronson *et al*. (1994) has defined an attitude as 'an enduring evaluation – positive or negative – of people, objects and ideas'. We can pick out two important features of attitudes from this definition. First, attitudes are long-lasting. Once we have an attitude to sport, we are likely to stick to it. Second, attitudes involve making judgements. Our attitudes to sport are likely to emerge as either distinctly positive or distinctly negative. Understanding attitudes is important to sport psychologists for a number of reasons. As parents and teachers, if we can understand how children acquire attitudes, we can use this understanding to try and ensure that as many young people as possible develop positive attitudes to sport. By understanding the link between attitudes and behaviour, we can try to help more people enjoy the medical and psychological benefits of both participation and spectatorship in sport. An understanding of the ways in which attitudes change is valuable in helping us to increase sporting participation and to motivate athletes.

The nature of attitudes

Pennington (1986) distinguished between two approaches to under-standing attitudes. The **functional approach** looks at why we have attitudes and how adopting particular attitudes can be helpful to us. The **structural approach** looks at which different factors make up atti-tudes.

The functional approach

Smith *et al.* (1964) suggested that having attitudes serves three main psychological purposes: the adaptive function, the knowledge func-tion and the ego-defensive function. The adaptive function of attitudes involves the usefulness of certain attitudes in helping us achieve our goals. For example, one way in which, as young people, we might 'get in' with a desirable crowd is to share their interest in sport in general or in a particular sport. This is not to say that people regu-larly and cynically change their attitudes in order to gain favour (although some people may do so on occasion). It is more likely that, without being aware of it, we are influenced in our attitudes by a knowledge of how much good or harm certain attitudes can do us.

The knowledge function of attitudes refers to the fact that having attitudes makes the world a simpler and more predictable place. It also means we can save ourselves 'mental energy' that would other-wise have to be spent analysing every person and situation we come across. For example, we might have a universally positive view of sport, regardless of the nature of different sports and the contexts in which sport takes place. Such an attitude then frees us from the complex business of making moral judgements about details such as safety, politics, etc.

The ego-defensive function of attitudes concerns the fact that we can adopt attitudes to help protect ourselves from difficult or painful feelings. For example, one way children might defend themselves against the feelings of humiliation they have experienced in P.E. lessons is to adopt a strongly negative attitude to all sport. People whose pride has suffered following a defeat in sport might similarly adopt a defensive attitude: 'I'm not bothered, I'm sick of basketball anyway ... '. As teachers, coaches and parents it is important to recog-nise how people use attitudes to make themselves feel better. We should not take someone too seriously if they say they are giving up their sport after a bad game. If, on the other hand, a player adopts an enduring negative attitude following a bad experience, we may wish to intervene to alter this attitude.

The structural approach

This approach looks at the different components that make up our attitudes. It is generally agreed that there are three aspects to our attitudes: the cognitive dimension, the affective dimension and the behavioural dimension. The cognitive dimension of attitudes concerns our *beliefs*. The affective dimension of attitudes concerns our *feelings* (in psychology the term 'affective' means emotional). The behavioural dimension of attitudes concerns our *actions*.

Applications of the structural approach to sport

Our beliefs are often stereotyped. We might, for example, hold stereo-typical views about those who favour particular sports. **Stereotypes** are beliefs that exaggerate the similarities of all members in a group and minimise the differences between members of the group. Thus we might mistakenly believe that all rugby players drink too much or that all football fans are violent. We also hold beliefs about the benefits of exercise and sport. Such beliefs are likely to have a strong effect on our sport and exercise behaviour.

It seems likely that our feelings about sport result at least in part from our beliefs. For example, if we believe that rugby players are always drunk or that football fans are all violent, we are likely to feel repulsed or frightened by them. We are also likely to have strong feelings about exercise and sport in general and about particular sports. Research has shown that the amount and type of information about a sport we give to students can affect their feelings about that sport. In general, the more we know about a sport, the more positive we feel about it. Theodorakis (1992) found that by increasing the level of technical information given to students on a skiing course, it was possible to make the students feel more positive about skiing. The relationship between beliefs and feelings and sport and exercise behaviour will be examined later in this chapter.

Boxing is a sport that most of us have a strong attitude towards, either positive or negative. Think about your own attitude to boxing.

1 Identify the cognitive component to your attitude, i.e. what beliefs do you hold about boxing?
2 Identify the affective component to your attitude, i.e. how do you feel about boxing?
3 Identify the behavioural component to your attitude, e.g. do you box or watch boxing?
4 How well do the cognitive, affective and behavioural components of your attitudes fit together?

Measuring attitudes

We can measure attitudes directly, i.e. by asking people questions or asking them to respond to statements that describe beliefs, feelings or behaviours associated with the topic we are interested in. There are other indirect ways of measuring attitudes (such as measuring physiological change or responses to ambiguous pictures), but sport psychologists tend to rely more on direct measures. Direct measurement of attitudes is done in three main ways: by Likert scales, by semantic differential scales and by Thurstone scales.

Likert scales

Likert (1932) developed the simplest and what has become the most common way of measuring attitudes. We start by producing an equal number of positive and negative statements concerning whatever we are measuring attitudes to. These statements can concern beliefs, feelings and behaviours. People are asked to respond to the statements, usually on a five-point scale, ranging from strongly disagree to strongly agree. Examples of statements measuring attitudes to boxing are shown in Table 3.1.

Table 3.1 Examples of Likert items measuring attitudes to boxing

		SA	A	?	D	SD
1	Boxing causes brain damage	❑	❑	❑	❑	❑
2	I watch boxing matches on TV	❑	❑	❑	❑	❑
3	I find boxing exciting	❑	❑	❑	❑	❑

You can see that Item 1 refers to a belief, Item 2 to a behaviour and Item 3 to an emotion. Thus cognitive, behavioural and affective dimensions are all included. Item 1 is a negative statement while the other two are positive statements. In order to score this type of test, you need to give all the positive statements values of 1–5, 5 being the most positive. For the negative statements you must reverse this, giving them values of 5–1. Each person who fills in the test can then be given a score for each item and finally an overall score which shows how positive or negative their attitude is.

Semantic differential scales

Osgood *et al.* (1957) developed an alternative procedure for direct measurement of attitudes. To prepare a semantic differential scale, you must first think of a number of words with opposite meanings that are applicable to describing the subject of the test. There are seven points between each pair of words. The respondent's task is to select a point in between the two extremes that best describes how they feel. Kenyon (1968) developed a semantic differential scale called the Attitudes Towards Physical Activity (ATPA) to measure how positively people feel about sport and exercise. The ATPA uses eight pairs of words opposite in meaning, referring to various types of physical activity and various functions of physical activity. Some items from the ATPA are shown in Table 3.2.

Table 3.2 Items from the Attitudes Towards Physical Activity scale

(a) Sport as a social experience							
good	1	2	3	4	5	6	7	bad
pleasant	1	2	3	4	5	6	7	unpleasant
wise	1	2	3	4	5	6	7	foolish

For example, in the three items in Table 3.2, someone with a positive attitude towards sport as a social experience would be expected to select numbers nearer 1 than 7 for each word-pair. The ATPA has been commonly used as a measure of attitudes to sport in sport psychology research. Simon and Smoll (1974) developed a modified version of the ATPA for use with children. Research using both the adult and child versions of the ATPA will be examined later in this chapter.

Thurstone scales

Thurstone (1929) developed a complex system of attitude measurement. Thurstone scales resemble Likert scales in that they appear as a series of statements to which the respondent chooses a response based on how closely they agree with the statement. However, Thurstone believed that it was important that we should know just *how* positive or negative each statement in a scale is, not just whether they are positive or negative. This is achieved by having a panel of judges, at least 50–100, rate each statement for positivity or negativity. The advantage of this is that, when we add up someone's scores, we can weight very positive and very negative statements more heavily than only mildly positive statements. For example, to return to the example of boxing, if someone replied 'strongly agree' to the statement 'There should be an immediate world ban on boxing', this represents a *more* negative view than if they gave the same response to the statement 'Boxing can be dangerous'.

Although, in principle, Thurstone scales should be more valid than Likert scales because of the weighting of items, in practice few researchers are willing to go to the extra effort needed to compile this type of scale. As Oppenheim (1992) pointed out, Likert scales generally produce much the same results as Thurstone scales with a fraction of the preparation time.

Pick a sporting issue, such as the danger of boxing or the importance of sport to children's development. Construct a mini-attitude scale using the Likert format and come up with 5–10 statements comprising both positive and negative statements.

The formation of attitudes to sport

How do we form the attitudes we hold to sport? Think about your own sporting attitudes for a moment. You may remember early positive or negative experiences that shaped your attitudes. You might be able to point to family members or teachers that were a strong influence on you. Did you take up a sport to impress someone attractive, or get into the in-crowd, and then find you liked it? You may feel that you are just the type of person that is naturally attracted to sport, or who is not. Actually, research has linked all these factors to the development of attitudes.

Personality, genetics and attitudes

Eysenck *et al.* (1982) proposed that people high in extroversion and psychoticism (see Chapter 2) tend to have pro-sport attitudes. This is because, to trait theorists like Eysenck, personality is primarily determined by genetics. We would expect that genetics may have an effect on attitudes. This is not to say that there is a gene for liking sport, but, if some aspects of personality are inherited, it may be that we can inherit a *predisposition* or a likelihood for developing certain kinds of attitude. Although there is a lack of direct evidence to support Eysenck's view that certain types of personality are attracted to sport, there is some evidence that genetics may predispose us to generally positive or negative attitudes to sport. Waller *et al.* (1990) found that separated identical twins (who are genetically identical) have more similar views on a variety of topics than separated fraternal twins (who share 50 per cent of their genes). This study implies that genetics plays some role in affecting our attitudes. However, we should remember that there are serious difficulties in conducting studies with separated twins – we never know for sure whether similarities between separated twins are due to similarities in genetics or environment. Actually, it seems likely that our childhood environment is more important than our genes in affecting our attitudes.

One reason why this approach to attitudes is not favoured in sport psychology is that it implies that attitudes are largely predetermined and there is little we can therefore do to intervene and shape people's developing attitudes. Actually, there is quite a lot that we as adults can do to influence the attitudes which children develop towards sport. The learning approach provides us with a number of techniques to give children positive attitudes towards sport.

Social learning of attitudes

As we discussed in Chapter 2, children tend to observe and copy the behaviour of their role models. Thus children are likely to copy the attitudes towards sport they see in their parents. Children also receive powerful reinforcers in response to the attitudes they express from a very early age. Social learning can help explain both attitudes to participation and spectating. We can easily imagine a scenario where a boy observes his father intently watching a football match and cheering when one team scores. The boy would be likely to copy the father's behaviour. It is also extremely likely that the father would respond to this by praising the boy and explaining the finer points of the match – thus reinforcing the behaviour. Using Bandura's four-stage model, this process is shown in Figure 3.1.

You may be thinking that this is a shamefully politically incorrect example: what about girls' attitudes to sport? Actually this was a deliberate ruse to make you think about how males and females might be exposed to different learning experiences. Imagine that in the scenario in Figure 3.1, instead of the son the young daughter of a football fan came in and cheered at the football. It is unlikely that she would receive the same positive reinforcers as her male counterpart. She might well be ignored – or worse punished. In our culture there are fewer opportunities for girls to learn the pleasure of sport spectatorship than for boys. The problem of gender differences in attitudes to sport spectatorship was highlighted during the 1998 World Cup, when the disparity between some men's and women's attitudes to

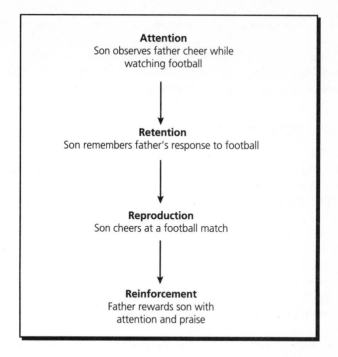

Figure 3.1 Social learning of a boy's attitude toward football

watching football became so opposed that the term 'World Cup widows' was coined, and *Relate Marriage Guidance* had to issue advice on how to maintain a relationship between two partners with different attitudes to watching football!

Girls may also be disadvantaged by social influences on their behaviour when it comes to sporting participation and performance. As compared with males, females tend to receive positive reinforcement for passivity, submissiveness, dependence, emotionality, low aggression and low need for achievement (Cox 1998). These influences are far from helpful to the young female athlete. Kremer and Scully (1994) have pointed out that apparently innocuous gender-specific messages such as 'don't get yourself dirty' can directly affect the developing child's understanding of her gender and so interfere with her developing attitudes towards sport. Despite these influences, however, research has generally failed to find any difference between girls' and boys' attitudes to participation in sport. For example, in the Hagger *et al.* (1997) study of English schoolchildren's attitudes to sport (see below for details), there was no significant difference between girls and boys on any of the subscales of the ATPA.

Attitudes to competition

Social learning theory is useful in understanding how we acquire our attitudes to competition. There has been much discussion in the last few years over British attitudes to competition. On one hand, it has been pointed out that the British may be less motivated to win than other cultures because of the philosophy of 'it's not the winning that counts, but the taking part'. On the other hand, concern has also been expressed that too much emphasis on competition prevents many children learning to enjoy sport. In one of the most comprehensive surveys ever of attitudes to sport, the Miller Lite report (Miller Brewing Company 1983), it was found that 86 per cent of American parents surveyed thought that physical education placed too much emphasis on competition. Gervis (1991) pointed out that problems can arise where early training overemphasises the importance of winning. This can be at least partially understood in terms of social learning theory. If reinforcement is only provided for winners, then by definition it is provided for half the participants in team games, much fewer in individual sports. With most participants failing to receive positive reinforcement, it is unlikely that the children will maintain their interest in sport. Table 3.3 gives examples of some ways in which positive reinforcement can be used by teachers and coaches to encourage positive attitudes to sport in all children.

Progress exercise

Think back to your childhood experiences of sport, e.g. P.E. lessons.

1 Did you generally receive plenty of positive reinforcement?
2 Do you think that you received most reinforcement for your successes, or for your participation and effort?

Table 3.3 Examples of using positive reinforcement to shape children's attitudes to sport
1 The amount of attention you give a child can affect their attitude to participating in sport. When coaching, give *all* children a share of your attention and help, not just the elite few.
2 Avoid separating off the weaker students and banishing them to practise separately. This lack of attention and encouragement will punish those children and prevent them acquiring positive attitudes to sport.
3 Give encouragement whenever possible. People will feel reinforced by the attention this shows.
4 Reward effort and personal achievement as well as more obvious successes. Noticing and acknowledging when a less able athlete masters a basic skill can affect that person's attitudes for life.
5 Punish lack of attention and effort, but never punish those who are trying hard because they lack ability. Don't forget that what you might see as a training exercise might be perceived by children as a punishment, e.g. giving the less fit extra fitness training.

Direct experience and attitudes

In addition to social learning, there is a simpler way in which children learn their attitudes: by associating sport with pleasant or unpleasant stimuli and feelings. This *learning by association* is called 'classical conditioning'. If we can lead children to associate sport with positive emotional states, they are likely to develop positive attitudes. One of the saddest effects of the commercialisation of football in Britain is that fewer children are being taken to matches. The excitement of seeing a football match live can provide a potent conditioning experience as the child learns to associate the positive feelings of attending the match with football itself. This is likely to give the child a lasting positive attitude to football. Without this type of experience, children's chances of acquiring strong positive attitudes to sport are diminished.

The other side of the association coin is that, if children come to associate sport with failure, humiliation or frustration, it is highly unlikely that they will develop a positive attitude. It is thus important that, as teachers and coaches, we take care to give children *positive experiences* of sport. This is particularly important as psychologists tend to believe that attitudes acquired by direct experience are the hardest to change. Damage done by poor coaching in the early years is thus unlikely to be undone.

What are children's attitudes to sport?

Given the emphasis in this chapter on the harm that can be done to children's attitudes by poor teaching and coaching, it is worth saying that (in general) research has found that children have very positive attitudes to sport. In one recent study, Hagger *et al.* (1997) surveyed 45 randomly selected 9–11-year-old English children on their attitudes to sport and found overwhelmingly positive attitudes. However, Hagger *et al.* also found that children with less positive attitudes tended to participate less in sport, underlining the importance of fostering positive attitudes in children.

Attitudes to sport and sporting behaviour

As Gill (1986) identified, we are interested in attitudes in sport psychology not so much for their own sake, as for their influence on sporting behaviour. A very important issue therefore concerns the extent to which attitudes can be used to predict behaviour. Early psychological research seemed to show that there was little relationship between attitudes and behaviour, but the current belief is that attitudes can effectively predict behaviour, provided we also have certain other information. In the Hagger *et al.* (1997) study, there was a significant difference between the attitudes to sport of children classified as high-activity and low-activity – supporting the idea of a strong relationship between attitudes and behaviour. Ajzen and Fishbein (1980) have produced a model of the link between attitudes and behaviour that has proved popular in sport psychology. This is called the Theory of Reasoned Action (or TRA). A simple version of the TRA is shown in Figure 3.2, used to explain participation in sport.

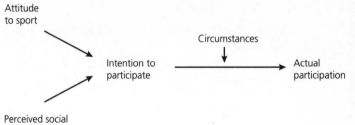

Figure 3.2 **Applying the Theory of Reasoned Action to explaining participation in sport**

In the TRA, two factors determine an individual's *intention* to take part in sport: their general attitude to sport and how socially desirable they consider sport to be. Therefore, before we even intend to participate in sport, we need to have positive feelings and beliefs about sport *and* we need to see sport as a socially desirable activity. Of course the intention to participate does not necessarily lead to the behaviour. Other circumstances may still interfere. For example, we might be particularly busy or plagued by a recurring injury.

Evaluation of the TRA

Generally sport psychologists believe that the TRA provides an excellent explanation of when attitudes to sport will predict sporting behaviour. Gill (1986) had students survey sixty-eight people on their attitudes to jogging. They then asked the participants how many times per week they jogged (as a measure of behaviour). A moderate relationship (r = 0.44) was found between attitude to jogging and frequency of jogging. However, as the TRA would predict, a much stronger correlation (r = 0.81) emerged between *intention to jog* and frequency of jogging. Theodorakis (1992) further confirmed that, as predicted by the TRA, as well as general attitudes to sport, social factors were particularly important in determining children's participation in sport.

1 What factors do you think might affect how socially desirable sport appears to an individual?
2 In what ways do you think we might make sport seem more socially desirable to an individual?

There are two main lessons to be learned from the body of research on the link between attitudes and behaviour in sport. First, if we want to accurately predict people's sporting participation, we need to know not just their general attitudes to sport but also their perceptions of how socially desirable sport is and any circumstances that might prevent them participating. Second, if we want to increase people's intention to participate in sport, we need to target both people's general attitudes to sport *and* their perceptions of the social desirability of sport.

Changing people's attitudes to sport

There are a number of theoretical approaches to attitude change. Perhaps the most famous and influential theories of how attitudes change are **cognitive dissonance** theory, proposed by Festinger (1957), and self-perception theory, proposed by Bem (1967).

Cognitive dissonance

Cognitive dissonance is the unpleasant sensation we experience when an attitude we hold comes into conflict with a current situation or intention. For example, we might believe that it is very important to work out at least three times a week, but we might not be able to work out for the next week, perhaps because we are going on holiday or working particularly hard. The belief and the intention are not compatible, so we would experience dissonance. We can deal with this dissonance in two ways: either by changing the behaviour (i.e. decide to work out after all) or by changing the attitude. We might use one of a number of rationalisations to change our attitude. We might for example think:

'It won't matter just for one week, especially at my age.'
'Too much working out was making me muscle-bound anyway.'
'I can't stand people who spend all their time in the gym.'
'I've missed weeks before and it hasn't done me any harm.'

Thus cognitive dissonance can explain how we can change our attitudes in response to new situations. We can also use techniques based on cognitive dissonance to deliberately influence people's attitudes. Gill (1986) gave an example of a P.E. teacher who used dissonance to alter boys' negative attitudes to skipping as an exercise. The boys started out thinking of skipping as a feminine activity. The teacher gave them a number of facts that were incompatible with their attitude, e.g. that boxers skip and that skipping is one of the toughest and best exercises. Faced with these facts the boys experienced cognitive dissonance and responded by changing their attitudes to skipping.

Evaluation of cognitive dissonance theory

Cognitive dissonance theory provides a way of understanding the ways in which we convince ourselves out of healthy behaviour such as regular training. Once we understand how we do this we are much less likely to con ourselves. Cognitive dissonance also provides us with a technique for persuading others to indulge in behaviour they see as socially undesirable. Looking back to Ajzen and Fishbein's theory, you can see that, as beliefs about social desirability are one of the main influences on our behaviour, techniques to alter these are extremely valuable.

Self-perception theory

A radically different approach to attitude change was proposed by Bem (1967). Bem proposed that our attitudes are determined by our behaviour. Bem used the example 'Since I eat brown bread, then I must like brown bread.' The implication of this is that we can change our own attitudes to sport for the better if we participate more and we can change the attitudes of others if we can persuade them to participate. Clearly, if someone holds strong anti-sport attitudes it is unlikely that we will succeed in persuading them to participate. However, encouraging participation among those who are not hostile to sport, but who have got out of the habit, may well produce significant alteration of their attitudes. Workplace football teams, community sports initiatives and fun runs can all persuade people to participate in sport, and hence develop more pro-sport attitudes.

Evaluation of self-perception theory

There is empirical support for the idea that changing sporting behaviour will affect sporting attitudes. Sidney *et al.* (1983) measured the attitudes of seventy-eight Canadian adults over sixty years old. The participants then took part in fourteen weeks of endurance training. The ATPA was then administered again and scores for each person were compared to those gathered before the training programme. The attitudes of those who trained the most were found to become more positive following the training programme, while the attitudes of those who trained least became more negative.

Clearly, self-perception theory can be applied fairly easily in order to change the attitudes of large numbers of people, via community and work-based sporting activities. There are of course two provisos to bear in mind when using this approach. First, regular participation in sport is much more likely to change attitudes than a one-off event. Second, participation must be an enjoyable experience. As you will know from your understanding of social learning and classical conditioning, people will learn positive attitudes from positive experiences and negative attitudes from negative experiences.

Summary

An understanding of attitudes can help us to develop healthy attitudes to sport in children and also to help change attitudes for the better in adults. The most important influence on our attitudes to sport come from direct experience and observation. It is therefore essential that we give children positive experiences of sport and encourage and reward their efforts. People's attitudes to sport are closely related to their participation in sport. The Theory of Reasoned Action has proved very useful in predicting people's sporting behaviour, based on attitudes to sport and perceived social desirability of sport. It has proved possible to change people's attitudes to sport, even quite late in life. Cognitive dissonance and self-perception theories have proved particularly useful in changing people's attitudes to sport.

Imagine you have been asked to give a school advice on how to encourage more of their pupils to enjoy and participate in sport. Based on psychological theory and research, suggest:

1 How more children could be helped to develop positive attitudes to sport.
2 How they might go about changing the attitudes of children not interested in sport.

Further reading

Gervis M (1991) Children in sport. In Bull S (ed.) *Sport psychology, a self-help guide*. Marlborough, Crowood. A practical guide to children's development of attitudes to sport and how to intervene. Good coverage of issues such as stress and competition.

Gill DL (1986) *Psychological dynamics of sport*. Champaign, Human Kinetics. Good general coverage of measuring attitudes and good coverage of research findings on attitudes to sport.

Pennington D (1986) *Essential social psychology*. London, Edward Arnold. An excellent introduction to social psychology. Particularly detailed account of both structural and functional accounts of attitudes. Good coverage of theories of attitude change.

Aggression in sport

As a society, we appear to have a certain ambivalence about aggression in sport. On one hand, as Russell (1993) pointed out, sport is perhaps the only peacetime setting in which we not only tolerate but actively encourage and enjoy aggressive behaviour. On the other hand, there is public outrage regarding football hooliganism and in recent years there have been a string of examples of athletes pursuing court cases against others who have deliberately injured them. One reason for this apparent ambivalence is that we tend to see aggression very differently in different situations. Before we proceed any further it is perhaps useful to look more closely at how we should define aggression.

Defining aggression

It is perhaps easiest to begin by saying what aggression is *not*. Aggression is not competitiveness, nor is it anger. Competitiveness is an attitude, anger is an emotion. While anger and competitiveness may both contribute to aggression, aggression itself is a *behaviour*. Aggression by definition involves actively *doing something unpleasant to someone*. Aggressive behaviour may come in many forms, ranging from verbal abuse – designed to cause psychological harm – to physical violence. It is generally agreed that all aggression involves the intent to cause harm in some form. Behaviour which accidentally harms someone is not aggression. Putting these factors together, a simple working definition of aggression would look something like this:

> Behaviour of any kind that is carried out with the intention of harming another person.

Hostile aggression, instrumental aggression and assertiveness

While this simple definition may suffice when describing aggression in most situations, things are more complex in sport. Clearly, when we perform a rugby tackle or a karate kick, we do so in the knowledge that we are inflicting a certain discomfort on the other athlete and that there is some risk of causing injury. This raises the difficult question 'Are behaviours within the rules of the sport that involve hurting another person truly aggressive?' Baron (1977) addressed this issue in his influential distinction between hostile and instrumental aggression.

> **Hostile aggression** takes place when the primary intention of the behaviour is to harm the other player. This type of aggression is accompanied by anger and the underlying wish is to see the victim suffer.
> **Instrumental aggression** takes place when the behaviour is clearly likely to cause harm, but its *intention* is to achieve a different aim, such as to score a point or prevent the opposition scoring a goal.

Husman and Silva (1984) have made the further distinction between aggression and assertiveness. **Assertiveness** involves the type of behaviour that might *appear* aggressive, but which does not result in harming an opponent. In many sports, for example, we might choose at certain times to charge directly towards an opponent, perhaps with accompanying shouting, but without any intention of charging into them. The classic example of this is rushing the net in tennis. Thirer (1993) pointed out that physical contact can be assertive rather than aggressive provided the intention is to gain dominance over the opponent rather than to injure them. Thus footballers can shoulder-barge one another while tackling, but, provided the intention is to obtain the ball rather than to injure, this is assertive rather than aggressive behaviour.

In contact sports, we generally accept a degree of instrumental aggression, although in no sport is it acceptable to cynically inflict serious damage on an opponent for the sake of gaining or saving a point. There is normally an elaborate set of rules in contact sports to make sure that moderate levels of instrumental aggression are permitted, whereas serious instrumental aggression and hostile aggression are not. Thus, although one footballer pushing another off balance would be unlikely to receive a card from the referee, high rugby tackles and low punches in boxing, which are judged likely to cause serious harm, are banned.

As Tenenbaum *et al.* (1997) pointed out, spectators as well as athletes can display both hostile and instrumental aggression. A crowd may hurl objects and abuse at players. If they do so with the aim of distracting the opposing team and so giving their own team an advantage, this constitutes instrumental aggression. If, however, it is done in anger and with the intention of harming opposing players, the same behaviour would be classed as hostile aggression.

Sanctioned and unsanctioned aggression

Apter (1993) has pointed out that there are often a set of unofficial rules as well as official rules governing what aggressive behaviours are acceptable. Thus a footballer committing a professional foul to prevent conceding a goal is committing **sanctioned aggression**, i.e. instrumental aggression that, while not within the official rules, is unofficially tolerated. The case of boxing raises particular problems for making a clear distinction between hostile and instrumental aggression, as the whole aim of the sport is to cause some degree of harm. Here the distinction between sanctioned and unsanctioned aggression is perhaps a clearer one. We would probably all accept that a boxer might lose their temper and try to hurt their opponent, but

Figure 4.1 **This England hockey player has a ferocious expression, but this is assertive not aggressive behaviour**
Source: Reproduced by kind permission of George Warwick

this would be sanctioned provided the fighter remained within the rules. If, however, they bit their opponent or punched to the neck or groin, that would clearly constitute unsanctioned aggression.

1 For each of the following sporting examples, all based on real-life events, decide whether the incident involves hostile aggression, instrumental aggression or assertiveness:

   (a) During a Test Match, bowlers consistently bowled bouncers in line with the batsman's body.
   (b) During a heavyweight title fight, a boxer bites off part of his opponent's ear.
   (c) A footballer consistently tackles over the ball, studs first.
   (d) A tennis player hits a forehand smash that glances off her opponent's calf.

2 For each of the above examples, consider whether the behaviour would be sanctioned.

The link between aggression and performance

It is commonly believed that the use of aggression wins games. The baseball coach Leo Durocher famously said 'Nice guys finish last.' In Tutko and Ogilvie's (1966) athletic motivation inventory, aggression was one of the ten personality traits believed to be associated with athletic success. Of course, we need to bear in mind the distinction between hostile aggression, instrumental aggression and assertiveness. It may be that the conventional wisdom supporting the value of aggression is in fact supporting assertive behaviour rather than aggression.

Young (1993) has noted the increase in unsanctioned violence in contact sports in recent years, and proposed that this is a direct result of increased professionalisation and the resulting financial incentives to win. But is there any evidence that aggression is really associated with good performance or the probability of winning?

Gill (1986) reviewed research on the consequences of aggression in sport. There has been relatively little research on this topic and almost all published research has involved ice hockey. Results regarding the link between aggression and success in ice hockey are equivocal. McCarthy and Kelly (1978) found a positive relationship between the time taken for penalties (a measure of a team's aggression) and number of goals scored. On the other hand, Wankel (1973) compared the penalty times of winning and losing ice hockey teams and found no difference. Given that ice hockey is such an aggressive sport, if no clear results emerge here, it is unlikely that aggression would be associated with success in other sports. Of course, as Gill points out, the situation and the reason for the aggression would make a difference to whether it was helpful. While the willingness to perform a professional foul would probably benefit a team, the anger associated with hostile aggression would probably be unproductive, harming concentration and decision-making.

Progress exercise

What has been your experience of aggression and success? Do you feel that you have been more successful when you have been particularly aggressive? Consider carefully whether your actions have been truly aggressive or assertive. Do you think your conclusions might be related to your particular choice of sport?

Theories of aggression

There are a number of psychological theories which aim to explain the origins and triggers of human aggression. Within sport psychology, three broad approaches have been particularly influential: **instinct** theories, social learning theory and the **frustration–aggression hypothesis**.

Instinct theories

In psychology the term instinct is used slightly more precisely than in ordinary conversation. An instinct is an *innate* tendency to behave in a certain way. By 'innate' we mean that the behaviour is in our genetic make-up and therefore present at birth. A number of psychological theories see aggression as instinctive and, at least to some extent, inevitable. In his early psychoanalytic work, Freud (1919) proposed that we are born with two opposing instincts: the life-instinct and the death-instinct. Our death-instinct leads us to be aggressive. Freud proposed that although the instinct to be aggressive is inevitable, we can still regulate it. Some contemporary writers, influenced by Freud, have viewed sport in general as a healthy way of expressing our death-instinct. For example, Richards (1994) looked at the importance we attach to kicking in expressing our aggressive tendencies, e.g. in phrases such as 'putting the boot in' and 'a kick in the teeth'. Richards suggested that football is particularly important in sublimating our aggressive instincts (i.e. channelling them constructively). For this reason, Richards describes football as 'a civilising influence'.

Another psychological approach that sees aggression as instinctive is that of **ethology**. From the ethological perspective, Lorenz (1966) proposed that humans have evolved a 'fighting instinct'. Evolution takes place through **natural selection**, therefore aggression must (historically at least) have been a **survival trait**, i.e. a characteristic that increases the likelihood of survival. Like Freud, Lorenz saw human aggression as inevitable but manageable. Lorenz saw sport as serving the social function of channelling human destructive instincts constructively. We shall return to the issue of the effects of sport on aggression later in the chapter.

Evaluation of the instinct approach

The issue of whether aggression is instinctive or whether we have to learn it remains an ongoing controversy in psychology. There is a lack of direct evidence for or against an aggressive instinct and we have to look to indirect support. If aggression were *universal* that would be strong evidence for an instinctive basis. Lore and Schultz (1993) have pointed out that all vertebrates display aggression, thus it must be a survival trait, as suggested by Lorenz. On the other hand, cross-cultural studies have found wide variations in human aggression (Baron and Richardson 1992). There appear to be human cultures, such as the Arapesh of New Guinea, where there is very little aggression by European and American standards. This suggests that there must be external influences as well as an instinctive component to aggression.

Social learning theory

In a radical alternative to instinct theory, Bandura (1973) proposed that all human aggression, like other social behaviour, is learned by imitation and reinforcement. Bandura (1965) famously demonstrated that children copy adults behaving aggressively in his 'bobo doll experiment'. Children observed an adult beating a large inflatable doll. Invariably the watching child imitated the behaviour and also beat the bobo doll. When the child was rewarded or witnessed the adult being rewarded for beating the doll, the level of aggression increased.

Clearly, there are instances where children can witness aggression in sport and there are a number of ways in which aggression can be reinforced. An act of aggression might result directly in scoring or preventing the opposition from doing so. Watchers might cheer, the coach and parents might praise the aggressive child. Children may also witness highly assertive acts and incorrectly imitate them in an aggressive form. You can imagine that, to a child with little technical knowledge of football, it is difficult to distinguish between an assertive shoulder-barge and an aggressive push.

Baron and Byrne (1994) suggest four aspects of aggression that can be explained by learning: how to be aggressive, who is an appropriate target for aggression, what actions require an aggressive response and in which situations aggression is appropriate. Thus, by **observational learning**, we might learn how to commit a foul, who we can foul, what they have to do to warrant a foul and under what circumstances a foul is the best response.

Because social learning theorists propose that there is nothing inevitable about aggression, but that it results from learning, it follows that we should be able to shape young athletes' aggression by the proper application of reinforcement and punishment. The alert teacher or coach can make sure that, while assertive behaviour is properly rewarded, aggression is not. We will return to the use of social learning to reduce aggression later in the chapter.

Evaluation of social learning theory

There is no doubt that children imitate adult behaviour and that rewards will increase the probability of aggressive behaviour being repeated. However, what is much more controversial is the claim that social learning is a *complete* explanation of human aggression. One question you might ask is 'If every generation copies aggression from the previous generation, how did it happen in the first place?' This is not an easy question to answer. Animal studies have shown that animals reared alone, without any opportunity to learn aggression from others, still display aggression. This shows that, in some species at least, aggression does not require social learning. Baron and Byrne's four aspects of learned aggression explain well the importance of learning in aggression. Nonetheless, we could see these as simply learning how and when to express our instinct for aggression. Social learning theory fails to account for findings (discussed later in this chapter) that, despite providing models of how to aggress, martial arts training reduces rather than increases aggressive behaviour.

The frustration–aggression hypothesis

This approach, first suggested by Dollard *et al.* (1939), sees the most important factors in aggression as the characteristics of the situation. In some ways, this approach resembles the situationalist approach to explaining behaviour (see Chapter 2). Dollard *et al.* proposed that, although we have an innate aggressive drive, aggressive behaviour is elicited by *frustration*, i.e. when we get frustrated we respond with aggressive behaviour. In the original version of the frustration–aggression hypothesis, frustration was seen as *always* leading to aggression and *all* aggression was seen as due to frustration.

Berkowitz (1993) has produced a more sophisticated version of the frustration–aggression hypothesis. Berkowitz proposed that frustration leads to anger rather than directly to aggression. More anger is generated if the frustration is unexpected or seen as unfair. Anger *may* lead to aggression, but because we can apply our higher mental processes (i.e. thinking, reasoning etc.) we do not *necessarily* respond to anger with aggression. We may do so, however, if our anger is great enough or if, for some reason, we cannot think logically at that moment.

Progress exercise

Under what sporting circumstances might you be unable to control your aggressive response to frustration? Think about when you might be particularly angry and about which other factors might prevent you thinking rationally.

Evaluation of the frustration–aggression hypothesis

Frustration is just one of several causes of aggression. Like instinct theory and social learning theory, it is an incomplete explanation of human aggression. Although the frustration–aggression hypothesis is not particularly influential in social psychology (Baron and Byrne 1994), it is useful to sport psychologists because sport can involve so much frustration that, even if frustration is a relatively minor cause of aggression in general, it is probably one of the major contributors to sporting aggression. Bakker *et al.* (1990) found that aggression increases when a team is losing, particularly when the game is of great importance, presumably in response to the frustration of the situation. Reducing the aggression associated with frustration will be examined later in the chapter.

Conclusions

Regardless of the accuracy of the *details* of these three theories, and regardless of the relative importance of the three factors emphasised by the theories, looking at instinct theory, social learning theory and the frustration–aggression hypothesis together does give us an insight into some of the major factors affecting human aggression. One way in which an innate predisposition towards aggression, learning of aggression and response to frustration can be combined to explain sporting aggression is shown in Figure 4.2.

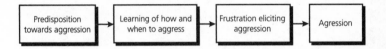

Figure 4.2 **An example of how innate tendency, learning and frustration might combine to explain human aggression**

Situational factors affecting aggression in sport

So far, in examining instinct theory and social learning theory, we have explained some of the major factors that underlie aggression in general. It is, however, also worth looking at some situational factors which have been shown to affect the probability of aggression occurring in sporting events. Of course some of these factors may cause frustration, fitting neatly into the frustration–aggression hypothesis. Some of the major situational factors are shown in Table 4.1.

Table 4.1 Situational factors affecting probability of aggression

Factor	Relationship to aggression
Temperature	+ive
Probability of retaliation	-ive
Point difference (if losing)	+ive
Position in league	-ive
Successful outcome in game	-ive
Crowd hostility	+ive
Aggression of opponent(s)	+ive
Source: Based on Leith (1991) and Cox (1998)	

Look at the factors in Table 4.1.

1 Which of these are likely to be a cause of frustration to players?
2 What other factors apart from frustration can you pull out of this list?

The $64,000 question: does sport increase or reduce aggression?

Instinct theories imply that, in general, sport serves to reduce aggression in society, because it gives us a legitimate way to express our aggressive instincts. The frustration–aggression hypothesis also supports the idea that sport is beneficial because it gives us a release for our frustrations. Most of us would agree that, if we are frustrated and in a bad mood, we tend to feel better if we exercise. Sport may also reduce aggression by helping us to acquire self-discipline. From a social learning perspective, however, we run the risk of learning new aggressive behaviours if we indulge in 'aggressive' sports.

The martial arts give us a way of directly testing these contrasting views. If the social learning approach is correct, we would expect the learning of aggressive repertoires of behaviour in martial arts training to increase levels of aggression. Research has shown quite the reverse, however: martial arts training appears to reduce aggression. Daniels and Thornton (1990) assessed karateka for aggression, using a test called the Buss–Durkee Hostility Inventory. They found that there was a negative relationship between **assaultive hostility** (reported tendency to respond with physical violence) and length of training (r = −0.64). Nosanchuk (1981) found a similar negative correlation between aggression and belt-level.

1 Do you feel more or less aggressive after sport? If the answer is 'it depends', then think about what factors it depends on.
2 Have you ever consciously used sport to calm down or get rid of your aggression?

Effects on spectators

While research cautiously supports the view that at least some sports help reduce aggression in participants, the reverse seems to be true for spectators – perhaps unsurprisingly given the problem of football violence. Arms *et al.* (1979) measured the hostility of spectators following aggressive sports (wrestling and ice hockey) and non-aggressive sport (swimming). They found increased hostility in those who had watched the aggressive sports but not in those watching the non-aggressive sports. Phillips (1986) tracked the rates of murder in the USA and found that, in the weeks following heavyweight title fights, rates of murder increased. The characteristics of murder victims appeared to be related to the losing fighter: when a white boxer lost, more white men were murdered, and when a black boxer lost, more black men were murdered. All the main theories of aggression could explain these effects. Instinct theorists would say that watching the aggressive sport aroused the aggressive instincts of the spectators but did not permit them a means of expressing their aggression. Frustration–aggression theorists could point to the frustration of having to watch the game and not be able to help one's own team. Social learning theorists might identify the modelling of aggressive behaviours by the athletes as the main factor in the increased hostility of spectators.

The reduction of aggression

There are a number of strategies that can be used to help reduce aggression in athletes. These approaches can be variously applied to preventing young athletes developing aggressive behaviour in the first place and curtailing aggressive behaviour in those prone to it.

Punishment

Punishment can be an effective tool for tackling athletic aggression. The effects of punishment are most easily understood in the context of social learning theory. The aggressive athlete can learn through punishment that the consequences of aggression will be negative. This is clearly most effective if punishment is implemented early in life – before the young athlete has received positive reinforcement for aggressive behaviour. Punishment can also serve as a deterrent. In social learning terms, the witnesses to punishment learn vicariously that aggression does not pay. Baron and Byrne (1994) suggest that to be effective, punishment needs to be prompt, severe enough to outweigh the benefits of the aggression and consistent. An example of prompt, severe punishment is football's red card.

Catharsis

Both instinct theories and the frustration–aggression hypothesis imply that 'getting it out of your system' or **catharsis** will reduce the need for aggression. Sport itself is cathartic, therefore we would expect that prolonged and hard training will reduce aggression. Baron and Byrne (1994) suggest that vigorous exercise can reduce aggression because it reduces both physical tension and feelings of anger. Although catharsis undoubtedly does reduce aggression, there are two serious provisos to its usefulness. First, the effects are temporary. If we start brooding again about what made us angry a few hours after exercise, we are likely to get angry all over again. Second, exercise in general is less satisfying and therefore less cathartic than hitting the person you are angry with!

Role modelling

If children can learn aggressive behaviour from watching aggressive adults, it follows that if we expose children exclusively to appropriate, non-aggressive role models, we can, to some extent at least, prevent them developing an aggressive repertoire of behaviour. This approach underlines the importance of the teacher or coach as a role model. Unfortunately it is almost inevitable that children will observe other athletes acting aggressively. Tenenbaum *et al.* (1997) suggested that the media are irresponsible in giving excessive coverage to, and sensationalising violent incidents in sport. Certainly, unless we prevent children spectating altogether – something that would probably kill their love of sport – it is impossible to prevent children encountering aggressive role models.

Contracting

One way of tackling aggression in persistent offenders is by the use of **psychological contracts**. Athletes signing a contract are committing themselves to eliminate certain behaviours. The terms of each contract are negotiated between the individual athlete and the coach or psychologist, but the contract will always specify which behaviours are to be eliminated under which circumstances. Leith (1991) suggests that a simple contract should include specification of the behaviour to be eliminated, punishment for breaching the contract, rewards for sticking to the contract, the names and signatures of both parties, and the date.

Think of your own sport and think of someone you know, or know of, who might benefit from a psychological contract. Draw up an imaginary contract for them, including all the details specified by Leith.

Progress exercise

Anger-management groups

We all experience anger and anger *per se* is not a bad thing, but it can lead to hostile aggression. If athletes are often becoming angry and that anger is consistently manifested in aggressive behaviour, they may benefit from anger-management groups. An anger-management group is a type of therapy group, in which anger is explored and mental strategies for better coping with anger are taught. Some groups – from the psychoanalytic tradition – emphasise exploration of the individual's anger, while more cognitive–behaviourally oriented groups emphasise the learning of strategies to control anger.

Summary

Aggression is behaviour intended to cause physical or psychological harm to another person. We can classify aggression as hostile or instrumental in intent and as sanctioned or unsanctioned according to its acceptability. While instrumental aggression under certain circumstances may help performance, hostile aggression is detrimental to performance. There are three main theories of the origins of aggression in sport. Instinct theory suggests that humans are innately aggressive. Social learning theory suggests, by contrast, that we learn to be aggressive from others. The frustration–aggression hypothesis suggests that we aggress in response to frustration. It seems likely that there is a strong element of truth in each of these theories and all can be applied to controlling and reducing aggression in sport.

Review exercise

Imagine you are a coach faced with a persistently aggressive athlete, who is puzzled as to why they are consistently aggressive.

1 Referring to the main theories of aggression, explain the likely causes of aggression.
2 Suggest some strategies for controlling/reducing their aggression.

Further reading

Baron R and Byrne D (1994) *Social psychology: understanding human interaction*. Boston, Allyn & Bacon. A good general account of aggression, pitched at undergraduate level. Particularly useful for theories of aggression and the reduction of aggression.

Cox R (1998) *Sport psychology, concepts and applications*. Boston, McGraw-Hill. Particular useful for examples of different types of aggression and theories of aggression. Also includes good coverage of the effect of situational factors in sporting aggression.

Kerr JH (1997) *Motivation and emotion in sport*. London, Taylor & Francis. Written from a reversal theory perspective. Particularly useful section on sanctioned and unsanctioned aggression.

Further reading

5

Arousal, anxiety and stress

Definitions of arousal, anxiety and stress
Factors inducing anxiety and stress
The relationship between arousal and performance
The relationship between anxiety and performance
Stress management
Summary

Common sense tells us that there are important links between sport and **arousal**, **anxiety** and **stress**. Sport normally involves competition which in turn tends to induce anxiety, characterised by an increase in arousal. You may have had the experience of performing better than you expected when anxious, or alternatively you might have had the less fortunate experience of making mistakes under pressure. Sport psychologists have been concerned with understanding which factors affect arousal, anxiety and stress, how these affect athletic performance, and how we can learn to regulate our arousal and anxiety in order to improve our performance. As Jones (1991) said, at the top sporting levels (at least in many sports), there is very little difference in the skill levels of the participants. It is thus often the ability to handle arousal, anxiety and stress that separates the winner and loser. Before going any further, it is important to understand exactly what psychologists mean when they use the terms arousal, anxiety and stress.

Definitions of arousal, anxiety and stress

Arousal may be defined as 'a general physiological and psychological activation varying on a continuum from deep sleep to intense excitement' (Gould and Krane 1992). When we are bored, relaxed or asleep we are in a state of low arousal. When excited, angry or anxious we are in a state of high arousal. You can see from this that being in a state of high or low arousal is not *in itself* necessarily a pleasant or unpleasant experience. Anxiety, on the other hand, is by definition an unpleasant sensation. Weinberg and Gould (1995, p.264) have offered the following definition of anxiety: 'a negative emotional state with feelings of nervousness, worry and apprehension associated with activation or arousal of the body.' We can thus think of anxiety as an unpleasant state of high arousal.

The term 'stress' has a broader meaning than anxiety. Stress is the process whereby an individual perceives a threat and responds with a series of psychological and physiological changes including increased arousal and the experience of anxiety. We tend to experience stress when we face demands that are difficult to meet, but which carry serious consequences if we fail to meet them. If stress is long-term, or *chronic*, it can cause serious harm to both physical and mental health. While it is quite normal – and as we shall see quite beneficial – to experience some anxiety before competing, an athlete should not feel constantly anxious and see themselves as facing insurmountable odds.

Somatic and cognitive anxiety

Martens *et al*. (1990) distinguished between two aspects of anxiety. When we are anxious we experience the physiological changes associated with high arousal, including increased heart rate and blood pressure, 'butterflies' in the stomach, faster breathing and flushed face. These effects are similar (though not identical) to the physiological effects of excitement and anger. We call the experience of physiological changes associated with anxiety **somatic anxiety** (from the Greek word *soma*, meaning 'body').

We can measure somatic anxiety directly by taking physiological measures, or indirectly by self-rating inventories. Direct physiological measures include urinalysis, galvanic skin-response and blood-pressure testing. Elevated levels of certain hormones released when we are anxious (such as adrenaline) can be detected in urine. We also tend to sweat more when anxious. This can be detected by a Galvanic Skin Response (GSR) meter, which measures the electrical conductivity of the skin: the more we sweat the better conductor our skin becomes. As our blood pressure also increases when we are anxious, this can be measured using a **sphygmomanometer**. There are two major problems with these physiological measures of anxiety. First, as we vary quite a lot in our normal physiological levels, every individual studied would have to have physiological measures taken over time to establish their levels with and without anxiety. Second, physiological measures require laboratory equipment and are difficult to administer in the field. Self-rating inventories can be used to indirectly measure somatic anxiety. We shall examine two such questionnaires, the SCAT and the CSAI-2 later in this chapter.

At the same time as we experience somatic anxiety, we also experience **cognitive anxiety**. Cognitive anxiety refers to the anxious thoughts that accompany somatic anxiety. Anxious thinking involves worries, self-doubts and images of losing and humiliation. A number of studies have examined how cognitive and somatic anxiety change before a sporting event. Swain and Jones (1993) followed forty-nine track and field athletes, measuring both the frequency and intensity of their cognitive and somatic anxiety on four occasions (two days, one day, two hours and thirty minutes) prior to an important competition. They found that both cognitive and somatic anxiety increased before the event, the most dramatic increase being in the frequency of anxious thinking immediately before competition.

Think about how you feel before an important competition. Write down some of the anxious thoughts that occur to you. At what point do you have most anxious thoughts?

Progress exercise

Once competition begins, it is commonly believed that somatic anxiety declines sharply, while cognitive anxiety fluctuates, depending on how the event is going. For this reason many researchers have proposed that errors during performance are due to cognitive anxiety and not somatic anxiety. Cox (1998) proposed that cognitive anxiety is negatively related to performance: as cognitive anxiety increases, performance declines. However, in the Swain and Jones (1993) study several athletes reported that they needed a degree of cognitive anxiety in order to perform well. You should bear in mind that it is very difficult to measure cognitive anxiety *during* sport, therefore we can only estimate the frequency and intensity of anxious thinking while athletes are performing. We shall return to the relationship between cognitive and somatic anxiety and performance later in this chapter.

State and trait anxiety

Another important distinction was made by Spielberger (1966) between **state** and **trait anxiety**. Trait anxiety refers to anxiety as an aspect of personality. A person high in trait anxiety will be consistently anxious, almost irrespective of the situation. In Chapter 2 we looked at Eysenck's trait theory of personality. Eysenck believed that some people were generally more anxious and moody than others because they were genetically programmed to react more to potential threats in their environment. Martens (1977) developed a self-rating inventory called the Sport Competition Anxiety Test (SCAT), designed to measure trait anxiety related to sport. Items from SCAT are shown in Table 5.1.

Table 5.1 Items from the Sport Competition Anxiety Test

	Hardly ever	Sometimes	Often
1 Before I compete I feel uneasy	A	B	C
2 Before I compete I worry about not competing well	A	B	C
3 When I compete I worry about making mistakes	A	B	C
4 Before I compete I am calm	A	B	C
5 Before I compete I get a queasy feeling in my stomach	A	B	C

Looking at the items in Table 5.1, you can see that they refer to both cognitive and somatic anxiety. A serious problem with SCAT is that, although it was intended to measure the *trait* of anxiety in sporting situations, because items refer to how the individual feels before competing it is likely that it actually measures *state anxiety* rather than trait anxiety.

State anxiety refers to the emotional state of anxiety (cognitive and somatic) typically experienced prior to and during competition. Martens *et al.* (1990) have produced an updated questionnaire: the Competitive State Anxiety Inventory-2 (CSAI-2), based on SCAT, which seeks to measure state anxiety before competition. Items from CSAI-2 are shown in Table 5.2.

Table 5.2 Items from the Competitive State Anxiety Inventory-2				
	not at all	somewhat	moderately so	very much so
1 I am concerned about this compe- tition	1	2	3	4
2 I feel nervous	1	2	3	4
3 I feel ill-at-ease	1	2	3	4
4 I have self-doubts	1	2	3	4
5 I feel jittery	1	2	3	4

During the early 1990s the CSAI-2 became the most widely accepted research tool for measuring competitive anxiety. It includes three subscales measuring cognitive anxiety (e.g. Items 1 and 3), somatic anxiety (e.g. Items 2 and 5) and self-confidence (e.g. Item 4). The Swain and Jones study discussed earlier in the chapter used the CSAI-2 as the measure of pre-competitive anxiety. However, the CSAI-2 has recently come under criticism, both for its phrasing and for its usefulness. Some items (such as Item 1 in Table 5.2) use the word 'concerned'. It is likely that all athletes are concerned about imminent competitions, so the answers probably do not tell us much about the athlete's anxiety. Collins (1998) has attacked research using the CSAI-2, saying that it is not a good predictor of performance and that it tells us little about the processes involved in the relationship between anxiety and performance.

Factors inducing anxiety and stress

How anxious we feel at any time is a product of both our individual psychological make-up and the characteristics of the situation we find ourselves in. When looking at why someone is anxious, we therefore need to take into account both situational and individual factors.

Situational factors

Event importance

The more important a sporting event is, the more stressful we are likely to find it. It is probably true to say, for example, that most footballers would find themselves more anxious competing in the World Cup than in a 'friendly'. However, we must remember that it is the importance of the event *to the individual* that counts. This does not necessarily depend on the status of the competition. For example, an athlete who knows they are being watched by talent scouts, or perhaps by their family for the first time, may feel particularly anxious.

Expectations

In the 1998 World Cup, it was said by many that Brazil had to cope with an additional pressure above and beyond those faced by other teams: the expectation of the world that they would win. It seems likely that in the end this contributed to their downfall. By contrast Croatia, who had far less pressure on them to succeed, exceeded all expectations by making it to the semi-finals. Individuals as well as teams can be adversely affected by the pressure of high expectations. Too much pressure from teachers, coaches and family can add tremendously to competitive anxiety. Of course the opposite can also hold true. An individual or team who believe themselves hopelessly outmatched by the opposition may find it difficult to get 'psyched up' and operate at too *low* a level of arousal.

Uncertainty

In general, uncertainty is stressful and the greater the uncertainty surrounding an event the greater the anxiety competitors will experience. Of course, if we introduced certainty about the outcome of sporting events there would be very little point in holding them! However, as Weinberg and Gould (1995) pointed out, teachers and coaches can remove some uncertainty from competition by making sure athletes are fully aware of procedures such as where to go and when, starting conventions, etc. In the same spirit it is important to ensure consistent refereeing so that competitors are clear on which actions are acceptable and unacceptable.

Individual factors

Trait anxiety

Some people are prone to suffer more anxiety than others, whatever the situation. This can be explained by genetics (see Eysenck's theory, Chapter 2), but also by experience. Social learning theorists might explain trait anxiety as having been learned from adults in childhood. The psychodynamic view emphasises the importance of early family relationships and the fact that those who experience early trauma or family disruption may afterwards suffer chronic anxiety. Individuals high in trait anxiety are likely to see competition as particularly stressful.

Self-esteem and self-efficacy

These commonly confused terms differ subtly but importantly in meaning. Self-esteem refers to how we *feel* about ourselves. Self-efficacy refers to our *beliefs* about our capabilities. Thus self-esteem is emotional in nature, while self-efficacy is cognitive. Both self-esteem and self-efficacy are related to our ability to cope with stress, low self-esteem and low self-efficacy being associated with high levels of anxiety when under pressure. In Chapter 7, dealing with motivation, we will look at ways of increasing athletes' self-efficacy in order to improve their performance.

The relationship between arousal and performance

Drive theory

Drive theory was proposed by Hull (1943). The theory itself is complex but its application to sporting performance is relatively simple. According to drive theory, three factors influence perform-ance: complexity of task, arousal and learned habits. The greater the arousal, the more likely we are to adopt the dominant response to a situation, i.e. our habit. Provided the task is *a simple one* and our dominant response is *the correct one*, the higher our arousal the better will be our performance,

i.e. performance = arousal × habit

This is shown in Figure 5.1.

If, however, the task is a complex one or the dominant response is not correct, arousal will inhibit performance. Because arousal level is greater in competition than in practice and increases according to the importance of the competition, drive theory would predict that the best performances take place in high-importance competition. Drive theory also predicts that, because expert performers are likely to have correct habits and novices bad habits, novices would be more likely to make mistakes under pressure. An important application of this prin-ciple is that if novices are to acquire better skills, they need to practise under conditions of low arousal (i.e. with minimal spectators and minimal competition).

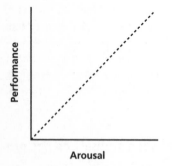

The greater the arousal,
the better the performance

Figure 5.1 **Drive theory of the relationship between arousal and performance for expert performers**

Evaluation of drive theory

Drive theory has proved extremely useful in explaining why experts do better in competition and novices are more likely to crack under pressure. It has also given us an insight into how to optimise athletes' arousal during training. However, drive theory fails to explain instances where even expert athletes become *too* aroused and make errors. It also fails to take account of the *type* of arousal experienced or psychological factors that may accompany arousal such as cognitive anxiety.

Inverted U hypothesis

By the 1970s psychologists were dissatisfied with drive theory and had turned to the inverted U approach to explain the relationship between arousal and performance. The inverted U hypothesis originated from Yerkes and Dodson (1908). The idea is that for every task there is an optimum level of arousal. Performance peaks at this level and drops off above and below it. This is shown in Figure 5.2.

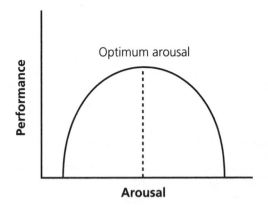

Figure 5.2 The inverted U hypothesis of arousal and performance

Progress exercise

Rank the following sporting skills in order according to how high you think the optimum level of arousal is for each.

1 A sliding football tackle
2 Bowling a slow ball
3 A tennis serve
4 Throwing a dart

The optimum level of arousal for a task depends on the complexity of the skill required to carry out that task. For a complex task involving fine motor skill (such as potting a ball in snooker), low levels of arousal are preferable. For gross tasks such as weightlifting, the optimum arousal level is much higher.

Evaluation of inverted U hypothesis

Like drive theory, the inverted U hypothesis has important applications in sport psychology. By looking at how fine the motor skills required for a particular sport are, we can then seek to optimise the arousal levels of competitors in that sport. Thus we may recommend relaxation procedures to lower the arousal levels of darts and snooker players, while recommending 'psyching up' exercises for weightlifters and rugby players. Unlike drive theory, the inverted U hypothesis can easily explain why expert performers sometimes make errors under pressure. However, like drive theory, the inverted U hypothesis fails to take account of the nature of the arousal or the effects of psychological factors such as cognitive anxiety on performance.

The relationship between anxiety and performance

In recent years the emphasis in sport psychology has shifted away from study of simple arousal in favour of looking at the more complex phenomena of anxiety. There are three particularly influential theories seeking to explain the relationship between anxiety and sporting performance: the catastrophe model, zones of optimal functioning and reversal theory.

The catastrophe model

Fazey and Hardy (1988) rejected the assumption of inverted U hypothesis that a small change in arousal will bring about a small change in performance. Instead they pointed out that when the athlete is experiencing high cognitive anxiety (i.e. they are worried), then a small increase in arousal beyond the optimum level can bring about a massive fall-off in performance. Figure 5.3 shows the relationship between arousal and performance under conditions of low and high cognitive anxiety.

Under conditions of low cognitive anxiety (i.e. when the athlete is not particularly worried), the inverted U hypothesis holds true. However, when cognitive anxiety is high then there comes a point just above the optimum level of arousal where performance drops off sharply. This is a catastrophe.

The catastrophe model has proved difficult to test directly. However, a study by Hardy *et al.* (1994) does support the idea that athletes' best and worst performances occur under conditions of high cognitive anxiety, and that under high cognitive anxiety performance drops off quickly following optimum arousal level. Eight experienced crown green bowlers were asked to bowl three balls at a jack on two consecutive days. On one day, prior to bowling they were given neutral instructions designed to create low cognitive anxiety; on the other day, they were given 'threatening' instructions designed to raise

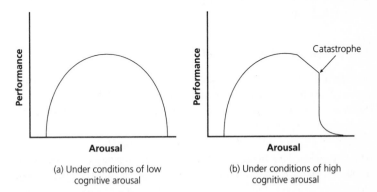

(a) Under conditions of low cognitive arousal

(b) Under conditions of high cognitive arousal

Figure 5.3 **Fazey and Hardy's catastrophe model of the relationship between anxiety and performance**

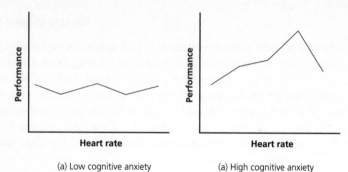

Figure 5.4 The relationship between arousal and bowls performance under low and high cognitive anxiety
Source: From Hardy *et al.* (1994)

their cognitive anxiety. The CSAI-2 was administered to confirm that cognitive anxiety was indeed higher following the 'threatening' instructions. To increase physiological arousal the participants were given shuttle-runs to perform and their heart rates were monitored. The results are shown in Figure 5.4.

You can see from Figure 5.4 that under conditions of low cognitive anxiety the results showed a weak inverted U, whereas under high cognitive anxiety performance peaked considerably higher but then dropped off quickly. This supports the catastrophe model.

Evaluation of the catastrophe model

The catastrophe model is more complex than the inverted U hypoth-esis and offers a more sophisticated understanding of the relationship between arousal and performance. The major practical application of the model is in showing that cognitive anxiety is not necessarily an enemy of performance, but under certain circumstances is beneficial (Hardy 1996). This fits in with the results of interviews by Jones *et al.* (1993), which found that many athletes reported that they performed best when worried. There have, however, been criticisms of the model. Gill (1994) proposed that it is essentially too complex to be entirely testable. Some researchers, such as Martens *et al.* (1990), have disputed the idea that cognitive anxiety can improve performance.

Zones of optimal functioning

Hanin (1986) criticised other theories of the relationship between anxiety and performance on the basis that they underemphasised individual differences in our responses to anxiety. When Hanin measured the pre-competitive anxiety scores of forty-six elite female rowers, he found a very wide variety of scores (mean score = 44, range = 26–67). Given the comparable success of these athletes, this variety of anxiety levels suggested there was a variety of different responses to anxiety. Instead of proposing a general relationship between anxiety and performance, Hanin suggested that each athlete has their own preferred level of anxiety and that their performance would suffer if their anxiety went below or above their preferred level. The athlete's preferred anxiety level is called their zone of optimal functioning (or ZOF). Figure 5.5 illustrates the differences athletes have in their preferred level of anxiety.

You can see that Athlete A has a low preferred level of anxiety. We might therefore refer to them as having a low ZOF. Athlete B has a medium ZOF and Athlete C a high ZOF. In general, athletes competing in team sports have a lower ZOF than competitors in individual events (Randle and Weinberg 1997). Athlete A is therefore typical of a team player and Athlete C more typical of an individual athlete.

The ZOF approach has clear applications for athletes. By knowing

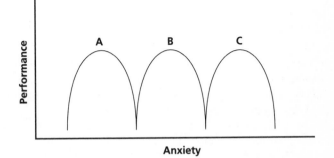

Figure 5.5 Zones of optimal functioning in three athletes

your own ideal level of anxiety for competition, you can monitor your current level and decide whether you need to relax or get more psyched up. Some athletes learn to monitor their heartbeat and from this tell whether they are below, in or above their zone. It is also useful for coaches and teachers to know individuals' ZOFs. You might, for example, choose not to use psyching up procedures prior to a competition if you are working with athletes who have a low ZOF and therefore prefer a lower level of anxiety.

Evaluation of the ZOF theory

There is some support for the idea that athletes do best when at the level of anxiety they prefer. Inlay *et al.* (1995) investigated anxiety levels in track and field athletes across seven competitions and found that, of athletes assessed as being in their ZOF, 63 per cent performed well and 31 per cent performed badly. This provides moderate support for the ZOF theory. However there are problems with this and similar studies. Pre-competition anxiety was assessed after the event rather than before. This means that there is some doubt as to the accuracy of measurement. Furthermore, Hanin did not differentiate between cognitive and somatic anxiety. In a more recent study, Randle and Weinberg (1997) used the CSAI-2 to assess cognitive and somatic anxiety of thirteen college-level female softball players and relate these to performance. No difference emerged between performance when in or out of the ZOF, thus this study did not support the idea of zones of optimal functioning. Despite these problems, however, Hanin's approach has many practical applications and is popular with athletes, coaches and sport psychologists.

Get together with a group of people who compete in sports. Each of you should rate on a scale of 1–10 how anxious you have been prior to the sporting events in which you have been most successful. This should correspond to your individual ZOFs.

1   Do you all appear to have different ZOFs?
2   Does there appear to be a difference between the ZOF of those participating in team and individual events?

Progress exercise

Stress management

Regardless of which theories of arousal and anxiety we would consider to be the most correct or useful, there is no doubting the fact that athletes' performance can be seriously affected by their levels of arousal and anxiety. There are a number of psychological techniques for regulating arousal and anxiety which can be applied to sport psychology. We can divide these techniques into three main approaches. Relaxation techniques are designed to reduce the athlete's arousal levels. **Cognitive–behavioural techniques** are designed to improve the confidence of the athlete and reduce cognitive anxiety. **Imagery** can be used in a number of ways, both to increase confidence and reduce arousal and anxiety.

Relaxation techniques

Relaxation means to reduce the body's arousal level. There are a number of ways in which we can learn to better relax. Two important ways of achieving relaxation are biofeedback and progressive muscle relaxation.

Biofeedback

One reason why we are not good at regulating our arousal levels consciously is that we have no accurate way of perceiving how aroused we are. The indicators of arousal (such as heart rate, blood pressure and skin temperature) are all very difficult for us to judge. The principle behind biofeedback is that if we can receive accurate information about our arousal level, we can learn to consciously control it. The simplest way to tell how aroused you are is to measure your skin temperature using a biodot. Biodots are small discs that change colour according to the temperature of your skin. The more relaxed you are the higher your skin temperature will be. By seeing the dot colour change as you relax and tense, you can gradually learn to relax or tense at will. Other simple ways of monitoring arousal include measuring the number of heartbeats per minute using a stethoscope and counting the number of breaths per minute. Of course as we all have slightly different heart rates, breathing rates and skin temperature, it is necessary before attempting biofeedback to establish what our individual levels are when we are relaxed and when we are tense.

There is a wealth of evidence supporting the effectiveness of biofeedback in aiding relaxation. There is also some evidence for its effectiveness in improving performance. Petruzello *et al.* (1991) reviewed studies relating biofeedback to performance and concluded that there was strong support for the idea that biofeedback using measurements of heart rate and breathing rate was effective in improving performance. A note of caution needs to be sounded at this point. While relaxation procedures such as biofeedback are effective in reducing arousal and aiding performance in over-aroused athletes, they should not be used without knowing that the athlete *is* over-aroused. There is little point in reducing the arousal of a relaxed athlete: you will merely send them to sleep!

Progressive muscle relaxation

This was the first of the modern relaxation techniques. Jacobsen (1929) proposed that, by relaxing each group of voluntary muscles, we can induce relaxation in the involuntary muscles as well. He developed a technique whereby each group of voluntary muscles is relaxed in turn. In the modern version of progressive muscle relaxation (or PMR), four sections of the body are relaxed in turn. These are (1) the arms, (2) the face, neck, shoulders and upper back, (3) the stomach and lower back, and (4) the hips and legs. Participants are taught to tense each muscle group before relaxing it, helping them to appreciate the difference in sensation between tense and relaxed muscles. A training session lasts about thirty minutes. Once athletes have mastered the techniques of PMR they can induce relaxation much more quickly.

The following is an extract from a PMR training session (adapted from Harris and Williams 1993):

'As we progress through each muscle group, you will first tense for approximately 5–7 seconds and then relax for 30–40 seconds. Do not start the tensing until I say "NOW." Continue to tense until I say "Okay".'

'Begin with tensing the muscles in the dominant hand and lower arm by making a tight fist NOW. Feel the tension in the hand, over the knuckles, and up into the lower arm. ... Okay, relax by simply letting go of the tension. Notice the difference between tension and relaxation ... Make another fist NOW. Okay, relax. Just let the relaxation happen: don't put out any effort.'

As with biofeedback, numerous studies have shown that PMR is effective in inducing relaxation. However, Cox (1998) reported finding no studies showing that PMR alone improved performance, although several studies showed that PMR combined with other techniques was successful in enhancing performance.

Cognitive–behavioural techniques

Cognitive–behavioural techniques for stress management, although only recently developed by psychologists, are rooted in the writings of the first-century philosopher Epictetus, who wrote: 'People are disturbed not so much by things but the views they take of them.' The principle behind cognitive approaches to stress management is that if we can make athletes perceive events as less threatening then they will not respond to them with the same anxiety. There are many forms of cognitive–behavioural therapy that can be applied to controlling competitive anxiety. In Chapter 7, which concerns motivation in sport, we shall discuss attribution training and self-efficacy theory. These are cognitive–behavioural approaches which help to increase confidence and reduce anxiety. Another approach of particular importance in sport psychology is Locke and Latham's (1985) goal-setting theory.

Goal-setting theory

Over the last decade the goal-setting approach has become popular in industry and education as well as in sport. The idea behind goal-setting theory is that, faced with the broad, general aims of whatever we are trying to achieve, we are likely to feel overwhelmed, demotivated and anxious. By breaking down the general goal into a number of smaller and more specific goals, we can make what we are trying to achieve appear less intimidating and more achievable. Thus goal-setting theory is both a theory of motivation and of stress management.

A rugby back might wish to improve their game. However, this broad aim is difficult to achieve because there are so many aspects to the game of rugby and because the size of the task is so daunting that it creates anxiety. According to goal-setting theory, the player should first identify one or two specific aspects of their game to work on. They should then set themselves small manageable goals for improvement. For example, a player might identify their tackling as an area to improve. They could then set themselves the highly specific task of successfully bringing down opponents 75 per cent of the time in the next game and increasing this to an average of 80 per cent by the end of the season.

There are two types of goal that can be set in sport. In the above example, the rugby back has set a **performance goal** (i.e. to improve an area of their performance). The alternative is to set an **outcome goal**. An outcome goal would involve winning contests as opposed to improving personal performance. This can create problems, as winning is not entirely in the control of the athlete. If an athlete set themselves an outcome goal of winning a match and vastly improved their performance, but was then beaten by a stronger or more experienced opponent, they would probably be needlessly demotivated. This illustrates that goal-setting is no panacea, but must be carefully thought out to be effective. Cox (1998) offered some guidelines for effective goal-setting:

1   Specific goals are better than general goals.
2   Goals should be measurable.
3   Difficult goals are better than easy goals.
4   Short-term goals can be useful in achieving longer-term goals.
5   Performance goals are better than outcome goals.
6   Goals should be written down and closely monitored.
7   Goals must be accepted by the athlete.

Evaluation of goal-setting theory

Broadly, research has supported the usefulness of goal-setting in improving performance. However, researchers have been divided on the importance of specific rather than general goals, and on that of difficult rather than easy goals. Weinberg *et al.* (1987) conducted an experiment on the impact of goal-setting on sit-up performance and found no difference in the performance of participants given moderate or difficult goals and those told to 'do their best'. This would appear to contradict goal-setting theory. However, 83 per cent of participants in the 'do your best' condition reported that *they had set themselves* goals. Thus success in this condition could be attributed to goal-setting. Weinberg and Weigand (1993) reviewed goal-setting research and concluded that most studies had found that goal-setting by an instructor had led to better performance than informal self-setting of goals.

Goal-setting has been applied to teams as well as individuals. Johnson *et al.* (1997) randomly allocated thirty-six novice bowls players to different goal-setting conditions. One group were told to 'do their best'; a second group were set individual goals; the third group were set group goals. After five weeks the three groups were assessed on their performance and those in the group-goals condition were found to be performing significantly better than the other groups. Interestingly, performance was no better in the individual-goals group than the 'do your best' group. These findings suggest that somehow teams respond powerfully to goal-setting, perhaps by increasing communication and cooperation.

Imagery techniques

Golfer Jack Nicklaus (Nicklaus 1974) once said that a good shot is 50 per cent due to the golfer's mental picture of what the shot should be like. The use of the 'mind's eye' or imagery is considered important both in stress management and in focusing athletes on their task. Imagery can be used in various ways to aid relaxation and focusing. Sport psychologists distinguish between external imagery, where athletes picture themselves performing *from the outside*, and internal imagery, where they view themselves performing *from inside* their own body. A good example of internal imagery is in the mental rehearsal of sporting techniques.

Mental rehearsal

Most of us that have ever participated in sport have, perhaps before a match, mentally rehearsed some of the actions that would be required during the contest. Mental practice of techniques does not necessarily involve imagery – we can mentally rehearse a tennis serve without visualising a tennis court and opponent in front of us. However, many athletes find that visualisation of themselves carrying out techniques is particularly helpful.

Mental rehearsal probably works for a number of reasons. The psychoneuromuscular theory emphasises the importance of 'muscle memory'. When we imagine carrying out a sporting technique, the nervous system and muscles react in a similar manner to that expected if we were actually carrying out the technique. This means that imagery helps us to learn and practice techniques. Another reason mental rehearsal works is that it **desensitises** us to the anxiety of competitive situations. The more we are exposed to things that cause us anxiety – whether in real-life or in our imagination – the less anxiety they cause.

Progress exercise

Imagine that you are about to compete at world level in your main sport. There is a packed stadium, the TV cameras are on you and you have been told how many millions are watching you across the world. Imagine how you would feel in each of the following scenarios:

(a) You have never done anything like this before, or even imagined what it is like.
(b) You are an old hand and have done this many times before.
(c) This is your first world-class event, but you have researched into exactly how the stadium will look and you have practised for months holding this image in your mind.

1 Rank the three scenarios in order according to which is the most and least frightening.
2 Given what you know about the relationship between anxiety and performance, which scenario is likely to have the greatest effect on your performance?

Vealey and Walter (1993) have described the use of imagery by the Soviet Union Olympic team in the 1976 Games. The team, who had never seen the Montreal stadium sites, were given photographs of the various sites so that they could visualise themselves performing *at those sites*. This may have helped the Soviet team to be less affected by the new environment when they encountered it.

There are numerous studies showing that mental rehearsal involving imagery is effective in enhancing performance. Grouios (1992) reviewed studies and concluded that mental rehearsal is more effective than no practice, although less effective than real-life practice. In general it appears that imagery is of most use to elite performers rather than novices and to those skilled in imagery.

Summary

Arousal, anxiety and stress are all separate, though related, concepts. All three can impact on sporting performance. There are two main theories of the relationship between arousal and performance. Drive theory suggests that the greater the arousal, the better the performance. The inverted U hypothesis, by contrast, suggests that there is an optimum level of arousal and that performance will decline above or below this. In recent years the research emphasis has shifted towards study of the relationship between anxiety and performance. Two theories have emerged as particularly influential. Fazey and Hardy's catastrophe theory suggests that, under conditions of low cognitive anxiety, the inverted U hypothesis holds true. However, under conditions of high cognitive anxiety, performance drops off sharply just after the optimum level of arousal has been reached. Hanin proposed that every athlete has their own zone of optimal functioning: the level of anxiety at which they perform best. This tends to be higher for individual than team sports. There are now a number of effective stress-management techniques that can be applied to sport psychology. These include relaxation procedures such as biofeedback and progressive muscle relaxation, cognitive–behavioural techniques such as goal-setting, and imagery techniques.

1 Distinguish between arousal, anxiety and stress.
2 Describe two types of anxiety identified by sport psychologists.
3 Compare two theories of the relationship between arousal and performance.
4 Describe one approach to stress management.

Further reading

Cox R (1998) *Sport psychology, concepts and applications*. Boston, McGraw-Hill. Covers similar issues to this chapter, but in more depth. Includes a number of studies seeking to test theories relating to arousal, anxiety and stress.

Mullins J (1993) Victory in sight. *New scientist* supplement. October, 4–9. Includes good real-life examples illustrating many of the issues and theories discussed in this chapter. Includes sections on biofeedback and imagery.

Williams JM (ed.) (1993) *Applied sport psychology, personal growth to peak performance*. Mountain View, Mayfield. Includes good chapters on several of the issues discussed here, including arousal–performance relationships, imagery and goal-setting. A particularly practical guide to the application of the approaches discussed in this book.

6

Social influences on sporting behaviour

- Sources of social influence
- Groups and teams
- Social facilitation
- Leadership
- Summary

Sources of social influence

We are all influenced all the time by other people. Perhaps our most important influences are those we encounter when we are children. The term socialisation describes 'the process whereby people acquire the rules of behaviour and the systems of beliefs and attitudes that equip a person to function effectively as a member of society' (Durkin 1995, p. 13). Probably the most important influence on our socialisation is the family. The term primary socialisation is used to mean socialisation by the family, especially by our parents. Other agents of socialisation include our friends, teachers and, in the case of young athletes, coaches and team-mates. The influence of these others is known as secondary socialisation.

Socialisation occurs in many ways. Social learning (discussed in detail in Chapter 2) is an important part of socialisation. Children imitate adult behaviour and receive a variety of rewards for doing so.

However, socialisation is more complex than just social learning. As children, we identify with significant adults such as our parents and coaches. This means that we wish to become *like* them. The quality of the relationship between the child and the socialising agent is crucial because without this the child will not seek to identify with the adult and is thus less likely to be influenced by them.

Coaching and socialisation

One of the most critical socialising influences on serious participants in sport, whether children or adults, is their coach. Terry (1991) has emphasised that coaching is more a matter of dealing with people than of disseminating knowledge. From a social learning perspective, the coach needs to be able to provide a role model, and to provide positive reinforcement for appropriate behaviour and reinforcement for inappropriate behaviour. However, perhaps more important is the ability of the coach to build good relationships with athletes.

Culture and socialisation

It is easy when studying psychology to look at socialisation in Europe and America and assume that what we see applies to all human societies. Actually humans live in a variety of cultures, which are quite distinct in the way they shape the behaviour of their young people. Triandis (1991) divided cultures into those that are primarily **collectivist** and those that are primarily **individualist**. More collectivist cultures (such as China and Japan) place a great deal of emphasis on groups, such as teams. More individualist cultures (such as Europe and North America) place much more emphasis on the individual.

The extent to which children are socialised towards sport depends to a large extent on the culture in which socialisation takes place. For example, Zaman (1998) has pointed out that Muslim women are excluded from almost all British sport. Zaman suggests that this is not due to any lack of desire to participate in physical activity, but rather because of a clash of cultures. The values of competitiveness, masculinity and confidence that dominate British sport are incompatible with Islamic feminine ideals. The Muslim Awarh (modesty of dress) is also difficult to cater for in anglicised sport settings.

Cultural differences in socialisation can also be seen in sport-related attitudes, e.g. towards cooperation, competition, achievement and winning. Research has identified Japanese children as socialised to be particularly respectful, cooperative and oriented towards achievement. All these characteristics probably serve to make Japanese children excellent team-players and extremely coachable. By contrast, North American children, while also very oriented towards achievement, have been found in many studies to be less cooperative and respectful of authority. This has clear implications for coaching. **Team-building** is a priority in Western sport, as cooperation and putting the team first cannot be taken for granted as they could be in a more collectivist culture.

Sport as a socialising agent

Sport is more than just a result of socialising influences. It can also be an *agent* of socialisation, i.e. an influence on the development of social attitudes, values and behaviour. A common assumption in sport psychology and in society in general is that sport and particularly *competition* is 'character-building'. Drewe (1998) identifies courage, dedication, discipline and perseverance as characteristics that are commonly believed to benefit from participation in sport. Danish (1996) has suggested that children can acquire valuable communication and decision-making skills from sporting participation.

Although there are certainly benefits to be had from participating in sport, we should be a little cautious about thinking that sport can only be positive as a socialising agent. There is little evidence that *all* children benefit from enforced participation in sport. Although it is probably true that many people learn many useful lessons from participating in competitive sport as children, we need to remember that some young people have almost entirely negative experiences of sport. Accounts of the benefits of sport almost inevitably come from those who have been successful in competition and have gone on to be successful in other areas (Krane 1998a), and there is a lack of research involving those who have had negative experiences of sport. It is difficult to see how a child who is left until last when teams are picked, and who always finishes last in individual sports, can learn anything except that life is harsh and that they are a failure.

Krane (1998b) has offered a balanced view of the positive and negative effects of sport as an agent of socialisation. At best, sport can provide good role models and be character-building. It can also provide positive images of minorities (such as ethnic minority groups and disabled people), helping to socialise young people against prejudices. However, as Krane points out, sport is rife with sexism. Women athletes who are heterosexual and appear to be 'feminine' are more positively portrayed in the media and are more likely to receive advertising contracts for endorsing products. Sport also tends to pit communities against one another. For example (although other factors apart from sport are certainly at work) cities such as Southampton and Portsmouth or Newcastle and Sunderland have traditionally bitter rivalries that are largely maintained by football clubs. In these cases, sport is helping to socialise young people into prejudices.

Groups and teams

Defining groups and teams

As social animals, humans spend a considerable amount of time in groups. A group has been defined by Moorhead and Griffin as 'two or more persons who interact with one another such that each person influences and is influenced by each other person' (Moorhead and Griffin 1998, p. 291). A team is more than just a group. Moorhead and Griffin define a team as 'a small number of people with complementary skills who are committed to a common purpose, common performance goals, and an approach for which they hold themselves mutually accountable' (Moorhead and Griffin 1998, p. 325). A team in the broader sense is not *necessarily* a group, because the members of a team can be working for a common aim without ever coming into contact with one another. For example, the British Olympic Team are clearly devoted to a common purpose, but they are not necessarily a group because they *could* fulfil their team roles without swimmers, boxers and long-distance runners ever meeting and directly influencing one another. Usually, however, when we refer to a team in sport psychology we are also referring to a group of people who play together and have a powerful influence on each other. For this reason, the terms *group* and *team* are sometimes used interchangeably.

Group formation

Merely placing a collection of individuals together does not in itself create a group or a team. Tuckman and Jensen (1977) suggested that when groups come together they go through five distinct stages. In the first *forming* stage, the group members get to know each other and basic rules for the conduct of group members are established. In the second *storming* stage, members compete for status in the group and group members take on different roles. In the third *norming* stage, the group settles down and group members develop attachments to each other and to the group. In the fourth *performing* stage, the group becomes oriented towards the task they have come together for and begins to achieve their goals. In the final *adjourning* stage, the task of the group has been accomplished and the group drifts apart. As Sutton (1994) points out, although this model of group formation is useful, not all groups operate in this manner. For example, in football, unless a new team is being started, it is unusual for a group to form in the way described by Tuckman and Jensen because new players join the team at different intervals. For an individual player joining an *existing* team, things are likely to be rather different.

Group cohesion

The word cohesion literally means 'sticking together'. Festinger *et al.* (1950) defined group cohesion as the sum of the forces that influence members in whether to remain part of a group. A highly cohesive group is likely to be more united and committed to success than a group low in cohesion. It is often said that a team is more than just the sum of the individual players. This is because the cohesiveness of a team can be just as important as the talent of individual team members. If you are a follower of football or rugby, you might have noticed that, in certain seasons, teams composed of brilliant individual performers collectively underperform. This is probably due to the fact that the team has somehow failed to 'gel' together. This is an example of lack of cohesion.

What determines team cohesion?

Carron (1993) identified four types of factor that affect the cohesiveness of a team. *Situational factors* include the physical environment in which the team meets and the size of the group. *Individual factors* refer to the characteristics of the athletes that make up the team. For example, the satisfaction of individuals concerning their being in the team can have a powerful influence on cohesiveness. The third type of factor is *leadership*: team coaches, captains and managers have a role in helping to make the team cohesive. *Team factors* include past shared successes, communication between members and having collective goals.

Cohesiveness and performance

There have been numerous studies showing that there is a relationship between team cohesiveness and success, i.e. more successful teams tend to have greater cohesion. However, what these findings do not tell us is whether the teams became more successful *because* they were already more cohesive, or whether in fact they *became* highly cohesive because they shared the experience of winning. It is quite possible that both of these possibilities are correct. Slater and Sewell (1994) measured team cohesion in sixty university-level hockey players – representing three male and three female teams – early, midway and at the end of the season. The researchers were able to see how early cohesion related to later success and how early success related to later cohesion. Slater and Sewell concluded that, while early success was related to later cohesion, the stronger relationship was between early cohesiveness and later success. They proposed that cohesiveness and success were mutually dependent. This is shown in Figure 6.1.

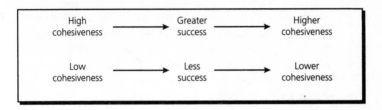

Figure 6.1 **The relationship between team cohesiveness and success**

You can see from Figure 6.1 that the cohesiveness of a team early in the season affects the success of the team, which in turn influences the cohesiveness of the team later in the season. It follows that one of the main priorities of a coach is to help develop a high degree of cohesion in a team.

Developing team cohesion

As we have already said, making a group of individuals into an effective team is an important part of a coach's task, particularly in individualist cultures such as Britain and the USA where we are not taught to put groups, of which we are a member, first. Strategies to develop team cohesion are known as 'team-building'. Carron *et al.* (1997) offer the following principles for team-building:

- each player should be acquainted with the responsibilities of other team members
- as coach, learn something personal about each team member and use it to gain cooperation ✓
- develop pride in the sub-teams within larger teams, e.g. the defence in a football team ✓
- involve players in decision-making to make them feel that the team belongs to them ✓
- set the team goals and celebrate when they are attained ✓
- teach each team member their responsibilities and convince them of their individual importance ✓
- allow team members to have disagreements ✓

- prevent the formation of cliques within the team, by giving every member opportunities to perform and avoiding scapegoating ✓
- use routines in practice designed to teach team members how dependent they are on each other ✓
- highlight the positive aspects of play, even when the team is on a losing streak ✓

Social facilitation

We have already discussed how being in a strongly cohesive team appears to improve the performance of team members. There are several other ways in which the presence of other people can affect our behaviour and performance. Under some circumstances the presence of other people, such as competitors, enhances our performance. However, under other circumstances our effort and our ability to make decisions can be adversely affected by others, leading to poor performance. The term social facilitation describes the ways in which our performance can be affected by the presence of others.

Co-action and audience effects

Co-action effects occur when other people are carrying out the same task alongside you, as takes place in a race, or when training with friends or team-mates. One of the earliest studies in sport psychology was by Triplett (1898). He found that children asked to wind fishing reels did so faster when in the presence of other children also winding fishing reels. Triplett also found that cyclists who trained with another cyclist practised at faster speeds than those training alone.

Audience effects occur when we are being watched. A study of audience effects was carried out by Michaels et al. (1982). Researchers observed pool players in a college student union and selected above average and below average players. First, those selected were watched and the percentage of successful shots was recorded. Four researchers then walked up to the tables of the selected players and watched the rest of their game. It was found that the audience had the opposite effect on the below-average and above-average players. The players identified as below average in ability played worse in the presence of an audience, while those identified as above average played better when watched.

Interestingly, it appears that audience effects increase as the size of the audience increases. Nevill and Cann (1998) examined the size of crowds in home-win games in the English and Scottish football leagues from 1985–96. It was found that the home advantage was greatest when crowds were large and least when crowds were small.

Explanations for co-action and audience effects

Drive theory

In Chapter 5 we discussed Hull's drive theory, which related arousal to performance. Zajonc (1965) proposed that the reason why the presence of others affects performance is because it directly raises arousal levels. Drive theory proposes that heightened arousal produces a better performance when the task is simple and/or the performer is an expert. Heightened arousal produces a worse performance, however, when the task is complex or the performer is a novice. It follows therefore that the presence of others will lead to a better performance for expert athletes but a worse performance for novices.

Evaluation of drive theory

The Michaels *et al.* (1982) study described above provides strong support for drive theory. Expert pool players performed better and novices worse when the researchers provided an audience for their game. Aronson *et al.* (1994) reviewed studies and concluded that there was overwhelming evidence for drive theory in that performance consistently improved in experts and declined in novices in numerous studies. A weakness, however, of Zajonc's application of drive theory is that he failed to explain *why* the presence of others should lead to increased arousal and how individuals might differ in their reactions to the presence of others.

Evaluation-apprehension theory

Cottrell (1968) offered an alternative to Zajonc's drive theory to explain *why* the presence of others might lead to increased arousal. In evaluation-apprehension theory, the presence of others causes an increase in our arousal because we feel that we are about to be *evalu-*

ated. If we are competent in the task to be observed then we are likely to feel confident and the effect of the observer on performance will be confident. If we are a novice, however, then the anxiety that results from the belief that we are about to be judged and found wanting increases our arousal levels and so spoils our performance.

Evaluation of evaluation-apprehension theory

Cottrell (1968) discovered that the more expert the observer of athletes, the greater the decline in the performance of non-expert performers. This supports the idea that it is fear of being judged that leads to increased arousal and poor performance. Certainly you can imagine that, if you found yourself watched by a panel of England team-selectors, your arousal level would be higher than if observed by a group of friends! On the downside, while evaluation-apprehension is almost certainly one cause of arousal in the presence of others, it may not be the *only* factor.

Social loafing

Audience and co-action effects occur when arousal increases. Under some circumstances individual performance declines when operating in a team, because arousal *decreases*. In the 1880s, French engineer Ringelmann discovered that when a group of men pulled together on a rope, each pulled considerably less hard than when pulling alone. When eight men were pulling, each person averaged half the effort they put in when pulling alone. This effect has since been demonstrated in a variety of settings, including team sports.

Knowing about social facilitation and **social loafing**, an obvious question to ask is 'How do we know whether, in a given situation, social facilitation or social loafing will occur?' Aronson *et al.* (1994) have identified two factors that affect which response takes place: the complexity of the task and the possibility of observers successfully seeing how much effort you make. If your individual efforts can be evaluated easily, you will tend to be highly aroused, therefore you are likely to do better on simple tasks and worse on complex tasks. If people cannot tell to look at you how hard you are trying, your arousal levels will tend to be lower, therefore you should do worse at simple tasks and better at complex tasks.

Progress exercise

1   As a coach, how might you avoid social loafing in team members?
2   Are there any circumstances under which social loafing might be prefer-
    able to social facilitation?

Groupthink

The presence of others affects us in many ways, not just in our arousal
levels and efforts. One other way in which we differ when alone or in a
group is in the way we make decisions. Janis (1982) identified the
phenomenon of **groupthink**. Groupthink occurs when group cohesion
is so great that it prevents group members voicing opinions that go
against the majority. Groupthink can cause serious problems for
teams, because the entire team can become so focused on a particular
goal that important considerations like practicality and safety are
abandoned. Janis described the symptoms of groupthink: the group
feels that it cannot make a wrong decision and that fate will support
them; group members decide not to 'rock the boat' by arguing with
the majority; those who do argue are made to conform or ignored.

Searle (1996) suggested that groupthink might have contributed to
the loss of six climbers on K2 in 1995. Three combined teams of
climbers continued to press on towards the K2 summit, despite clearly
dangerous and worsening conditions. This resulted in the deaths of
six climbers. One of the survivors was quoted as saying 'the most
dangerous thing about groups is that everyone hands over responsibility for themselves to someone else.' It appears that, because of the
desire to complete the expedition, the group went into groupthink
and ignored the danger.

Leadership

Leadership was defined by Moorhead and Griffin as 'the use of nonco-
ercive influence to direct and coordinate the activities of group
members to meet a goal' (Moorhead and Griffin 1998, p. 352).

95

Leadership may be informal or formal. When we appoint a team coach and a captain, we know that they have formal leadership roles. However, other team members might also take on informal roles in which they influence and inspire others. For many years psychologists have been concerned with who become leaders and how they carry out their role. In the remainder of this chapter we shall examine both of these issues.

Leadership style

There is more than one way to lead people. An early but still influential distinction is between authoritarian, *laissez-faire* and democratic styles of leadership (Lewin *et al.* 1939). The *authoritarian* leader makes decisions alone and expects unquestioning obedience from the group. This approach has advantages and disadvantages in sport. The main advantage is that team members can still be directed towards purposeful action when they are exhausted, stressed and disillusioned. However, authoritarian leadership has its costs. Other team members are often denied what would be useful input to decision-making and, in the absence of the leader, the group may have difficulty in motivating themselves.

By contrast, the *laissez-faire* leader leaves group members to get on with the task at hand without interference. They may assist individuals but do not attempt to organise or motivate the group as a whole. While being a member of a group with *laissez-faire* leadership might allow you to explore your talents without being unnecessarily restricted, leaders who can *only* operate in a *laissez-faire* manner often fail to motivate groups to achieve their potential or cope with crises.

Lewin's third category of leader, the *democratic* leader may be seen as a halfway position between authoritarian and *laissez-faire* styles. The democratic leader takes decisions and enforces them, but decisions always take account of the views of the rest of the group. Democratic leadership can cause difficulties when very rapid decision-making is required in an emergency, but in most cases this is the most successful style of leadership.

Lewin has offered a useful approach to understanding how leaders may operate. This does not mean, however, that a leader can only operate in one way. Lewin believed that each style of leadership works in different situations and that the best leaders can use all three styles as appropriate.

Theories of leadership

Trait theories

Early psychological approaches to leadership emphasised the importance of being a certain type of person, i.e. having certain *personality traits* (see Chapter 2), in order to be a good leader. This 'great person' approach depends on three main assumptions. First, all successful leaders have certain personality traits in common. Second, the rest of us 'mere mortals' do not share the characteristics of great leaders. Third, the traits that make someone a leader in one situation will also enable them to lead successfully in quite different situations. Researchers have attempted for many years to find out which traits make a good leader. Although there appears to be no set of personality traits that are necessary to be leader, there are certain characteristics that are found in a large number of successful leaders and which appear to be helpful in leading others. Kirkpatrick and Locke (1991) identified eight characteristics which are associated with successful leadership. These are drive (ambition and persistence), honesty, motivation to lead, self-confidence, intelligence, expertise in the purpose of the group, creativity (imagination and originality) and flexibility. Kirkpatrick and Locke concluded that 'leaders do not have to be great men or women by being intellectual geniuses or omniscient prophets, but they do need to have the "right stuff" and this stuff is not equally present in all people' (Kirkpatrick and Locke 1991, p. 58).

Evaluation of trait theories

The trait approach has failed to identify a combination of personality traits that will invariably lead to a person becoming a successful leader. However, it has been quite successful in the more modest aim of identifying characteristics that are likely to be *helpful* to leaders. Looking at Kirkpatrick and Locke's list of characteristics associated with successful leadership, you can see how it might be useful to bear these in mind when choosing a leader, e.g. a team captain. If someone you are considering as captain lacks a number of these attributes, it is perhaps unlikely that they will turn out to be a good choice. The main problem with the trait approach is that it neglects the importance of the *situation* in which the leader is operating. Different leaders do best in different circumstances. In the next theory we shall look at, Fiedler has aimed to explain how leaders might be matched to their particular task.

Progress exercise

Think of sporting leaders you have contact with, such as your coach, team captain, etc.

1   Are they effective leaders?
2   If so, what personal characteristics do you think are particularly helpful to them?

Fiedler's contingency theory

According to contingency theory, the success of leadership depends on the characteristics of the leader *and* the situation in which they are leading. Fiedler (1967) identified two categories of leader: those who are task-oriented (i.e. their main preoccupation is the *task* of the group) and those who are person-oriented (i.e. their main preoccupation is the *members* of the group). Fiedler developed a way of distinguishing task-oriented and person-oriented leaders, asking them by means of a questionnaire about their least effective team member or (to use Fiedler's terms) *Least-Preferred Coworker* (LPC). Those who hold the LPC in low esteem are assumed to be task-oriented, because they are thinking first of the likelihood of accomplishing their task while handicapped by the ineffective team member; those who hold the LPC in high esteem are assumed to be person-oriented, because they are valuing the team member despite their lack of contribution to achieving the task at hand.

Fiedler proposed that task-oriented and person-oriented leaders are effective under different circumstances. Under very favourable or very unfavourable circumstances, task-oriented leaders get better results. Favourable conditions occur when there is a clearly defined task, good leader–group relations and the leader has the power to enforce their decisions. Under moderately favourable conditions, person-oriented leaders are more effective.

Evaluation of Fiedler's theory

Fiedler has contributed to our understanding of leadership by showing how the personality of the leader and the situation in which they are leading are both important to how successful leadership is. Cox (1998) has pointed out that there are a number of cases in sport which demonstrate how leaders with particular personalities have been very successful under some circumstances and unsuccessful in a different situation. You only have to look at the changing fortunes of British football managers, such as the former England manager Graham Taylor, to see that this principle of Fiedler's theory is valid. However, more questionable are the *specifics* of Fiedler's theory. Gill (1986) reviewed research into the effects of situation and leader-personality in sports teams, and concluded that results were inconclusive.

Summary

We are all influenced by others. As children, we are *socialised* in sporting behaviour, influenced by family, friends, team-mates, teachers and coaches. The culture in which we grow up plays a crucial role in the nature of the socialisation process. Sport is not only a product of socialisation, but also an important *agent* of socialisation, i.e. participating in sport is likely to have important effects on our development. Our behaviour and our performance is also influenced by membership of groups and teams. Team cohesion appears to be particularly important in affecting our performance. The presence of others, whether as competitors, spectators or team-mates, can have a variety of *social facilitation* effects, i.e. effects both positive and negative on our performance. Leaders can have a profound effect on the way teams behave and perform. There are different styles of leadership and different types of leader are effective under different circumstances. However, certain personality traits seem to be helpful in effective leadership.

Review exercise

Think of a team you play in or have played in:

1 What effects do you think membership of this team might have had on your character?
2 How cohesive is/was this team? What effects might this have had on its performance?
3 How has this team performed in competition and in front of an audience, as opposed to alone in training?
4 Think of the team leaders, e.g. captain, coach. What styles have they used and how effective have they been?

Further reading

Baron R and Byrne D (1994) *Social psychology: understanding human interaction*. Boston, Allyn & Bacon. An advanced social psychology text, with detailed coverage of social facilitation and leadership.

Cox R (1998) *Sport psychology, concepts and applications*. Boston, McGraw-Hill. Detailed coverage with examples of most of the issues covered in this chapter.

Williams JM (ed.) (1993) *Applied sport psychology, personal growth to peak performance*. Mountain View, Mayfield. Includes several chapters on groups and leadership. Lots of practical information for those leading sports teams and groups.

7

Motivation and sport

Intrinsic and extrinsic motivation
Humanistic perspectives on motivation
Achievement-motivation
Cognitive approaches to motivation
Contemporary research on motives for sports participation
Summary

One of the fundamental questions psychologists need to address about human nature is 'Why do we do things?' We could simply answer 'Because I want to', 'Because I need to' or even 'Because I just do'. However, although all these statements are useful starting points, psychologists are not satisfied with these answers and seek to uncover the reasons *underlying* our experiences of wanting to, needing to or 'just doing' things. In this chapter, we will examine some basic types of human motivation, theories about specific motivators and research findings concerning what motivates us to participate and succeed in sport. A useful starting point is to examine intrinsic and extrinsic motivation.

Intrinsic and extrinsic motivation

An important distinction in types of human motives is between extrinsic and intrinsic motivation. Extrinsic motivation results from external rewards; intrinsic motivation comes from within the person. Both external and intrinsic motives are important in sport and sport psychologists can work with both extrinsic and intrinsic motives to improve the performance of the individual. Intrinsic motives for taking part in sport include excitement, fun, love of action and the chance to demonstrate and improve our skills – in short, all the reasons we *enjoy* sport. Later in this chapter we will discuss some techniques designed to increase intrinsic motivation. The reason these can be used so effectively to motivate athletes is that they directly affect our intrinsic motivation. Extrinsic motives can come in the form of trophies, prizes and less tangible rewards such as praise and status.

Generally, we tend to come to sport motivated more by intrinsic than extrinsic factors. However, extrinsic motivators have been used in an attempt to boost intrinsic motivation. The *additive principle* states that an athlete low in intrinsic motivation can have their motivation boosted by adding some extrinsic motivation. This common-sense approach has, however, not been well supported by research. There are numerous case studies of athletes whose performance has sharply declined as soon as they have received lucrative contracts (Cox 1998). Intensive, stressful competition may also reduce intrinsic motivation. Fortier *et al.* (1995) compared the intrinsic motivation levels of Canadian athletes who participated for recreation with those involved in collegiate competition. The collegiate athletes, who were highly focused on the goal of winning, showed less intrinsic motivation than those participating for pleasure.

One example of how extrinsic motivators can be used successfully to boost intrinsic motivation is in the grading systems of the Eastern martial arts, usually symbolised by a coloured belt or sash. Contrary to popular belief, belts are not an ancient tradition but a relatively recent innovation in the martial arts. They are designed to provide regular tangible rewards for students' achievements, with the aim of motivating students to continue.

Humanistic perspectives on motivation

Maslow's theory of needs

Maslow (1954) developed a theory of human motivation that aimed to explain all the types of human need and rank them in the order

Figure 7.1 **Maslow's hierarchy of needs**

people seek to satisfy them. Maslow's hierarchy of needs is shown in Figure 7.1.

The idea behind the hierarchy of needs is that we ascend the hierarchy, satisfying each motive in turn. Our first priority is to satisfy our *physiological needs*, such as for food and warmth, because we cannot live without these. Only when these needs have been satisfied do we seek out *safety*. Once we are safe, the next thing we need to worry about is our *social needs*, i.e. to belong to a group and have relationships with others. When our social needs are satisfied then *esteem needs* will become paramount. To satisfy our esteem needs, we need to achieve, become competent and be recognised as such. Once this has been achieved our focus will shift to satisfying our *intellectual needs*. Intellectual needs include gaining understanding and knowledge. Next in Maslow's hierarchy come *aesthetic needs*, i.e. the need for beauty, order and balance. The final human need identified by Maslow is for *self-actualisation*, i.e. to find personal fulfilment and achieve one's potential.

According to Maslow, we are all striving to ascend the hierarchy of needs, but very few of us achieve self-actualisation. Sport, however, does provide a possible path to self-actualisation. Athletes who rise to the very top of their field, holding world records and championship titles, could be said to be self-actualised in that they have fulfilled their dreams and their potential. On the other hand, we should be careful not to equate self-actualisation with success. There are numerous sporting celebrities who, despite rising to the top of their chosen sport and appearing to fulfil their potential, have clearly not found personal fulfilment and have, by contrast, 'gone off the rails'.

Progress exercise

1 Using a spider diagram, brainstorm as many reasons as you can think of for doing sport.
2 Fit all these reasons into Maslow's hierarchy of needs, as shown in Figure 7.2.

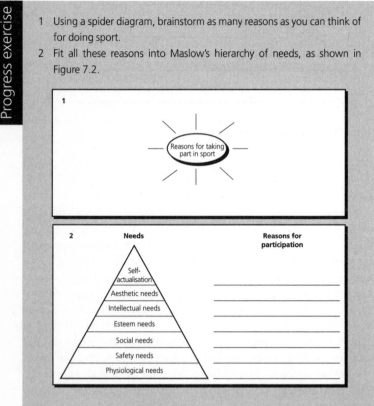

Figure 7.2 **Fitting reasons for sports participation into the hierarchy of needs**

3 At what level in the hierarchy are most of your reasons for sporting
   participation?
4 Most people's responses tend to be around the social and esteem levels.
   Why do you think this might be and whose responses might tend to be
   higher up the hierarchy?

Evaluation of Maslow's theory

Maslow's theory has been enormously influential. Most importantly, he has opened our eyes to the *range* of human needs. If you have carried out the exercise above, you have probably seen that you have multiple reasons for participating in sport and that your reasons are grouped above the physiological and safety needs. If you are motivated principally by physiological and safety needs (say, for example, if you are homeless and starving) it is unlikely that you would be able to raise much motivation to take part in sport. Sport is an excellent way of providing for our esteem and social needs. For some, it may also provide a path to self-actualisation.

Despite the usefulness of Maslow's work, his prediction that we are all motivated by these needs and that everybody seeks to satisfy them in the same order is suspect, particularly when we look at elite athletes who have put success ahead of other considerations. Saul (1993) has pointed out that 65 per cent of ballet dancers have chronic injuries and suggested that they have sacrificed physiological needs in pursuit of aesthetic needs. This is perhaps an extreme example, but it illustrates that sometimes aiming for higher needs means not satisfying the more basic needs – contrary to Maslow's theory.

Achievement-motivation

The link between the wish to achieve and sporting success is an obvious one. A strong wish to succeed in your chosen sport will be a huge asset in determining how hard you train and how hard you try in competition. All participation in sport involves achievement, regardless of whether you regard competition as important. You are in fact probably more likely to boost your performance by setting yourself goals of personal achievement (e.g. 90 per cent of first serves in, 80 per cent of penalties in the net), rather than goals of victory (see the section on goal-setting in Chapter 5). Some psychologists see the drive to achieve as innate, whereas others see it as acquired by experience. Some believe that the most important factor is to achieve success whereas others emphasise the motive to avoid failure. The most influential theory of achievement-motivation comes from McClelland *et al.* (1953).

The McClelland–Atkinson theory of need achievement

The aim of McClelland and Atkinson's theory was to explain why some individuals are more motivated to achieve than others. The athlete's intrinsic motivation is seen as the motive to achieve. Acting against this intrinsic motivation, however, is the motive to avoid failure. When faced with a task such as sport, we face an approach-avoidance conflict. We are motivated to approach and take part by our desire to succeed, but we are also motivated to avoid taking part by our desire to avoid failure. Our individual decision to participate in sport is determined by the relative strength of these two factors. This can be shown in an equation.

achievement-motivation = desire to succeed − fear of failure

To McClelland and Atkinson, achievement-motivation is a personality trait. For some of us, the desire to succeed far outweighs the fear of failure and we are said to be high in achievement-motivation. For others, the fear of failure is the more important factor and they would be said to be low in achievement-motivation. This personality trait is not the only factor that affects motivation. The situation is also important, specifically the *probability of success* and the *incentive for success*. Thus, even if an athlete is low in achievement-motivation, if the probability of success is high, and the rewards for success are great, they are likely to be motivated.

Evaluation of McClelland and Atkinson's theory

Gill (1986) reviewed research on choice of high and low difficulty tasks and concluded that there is much support for the prediction of the theory that high achievers seek out difficult tasks and low achievers prefer easier tasks. However, the theory does not reliably predict sporting *performance*. This does not mean, of course, that the theory is worthless. Cox (1998) points out that the value of measuring achievement-motivation is not to predict performance, but to predict long-term patterns of motivation.

Fear of success

From the earliest studies of achievement-motivation, it became apparent that there were gender differences. This has been confirmed in contemporary studies, such as those of Ashford *et al.* (1993) and Daley and O'Gara (1998), considered later in this chapter. Horner (1972) proposed that gender differences in achievement-motivation could be explained by a third motive that complemented the motive to succeed and the motive to avoid failure of the McClelland–Atkinson theory. This third motive was termed fear of success (FOS). This motive acts against the desire to succeed and desire to avoid failure. Horner suggested that, although women have an equal desire to achieve and desire to avoid failure, they differ from men in achievement-motivation because of their greater fear of success.

Evaluation of FOS theory

Research following Horner's work has yielded contradictory results. Although fear of success appears to be a valid idea, some researchers have found that it is equally common in men, hence it may not be an explanation of gender differences in achievement-motivation. A further problem lies with the scale Horner designed to measure FOS. It is possible that responses to FOS items are affected not only by women's own feelings, but also by their stereotyped beliefs about women and success.

Cognitive approaches to motivation

Whereas the humanistic approach to motivation is holistic (i.e. it attempts to explain human experience in its entirety), the cognitive approach focuses specifically on one aspect of human experience:

how we *think*. Sport psychologists have been particularly interested in two aspects of how we think: **attribution** and self-efficacy.

Attribution

Because humans have a desire to try to understand the world around us, we have a powerful tendency to make attributions about the causes of events and behaviour. This means that we come to a conclusion about *why* something happened or *why* someone behaved or performed in a certain way. We make attributions about our own behaviour and about the behaviour of those around us, *whether or not we have the evidence to arrive at accurate conclusions*. In this chapter we are chiefly concerned with the attributions we make about ourselves.

Internal and external attributions

Broadly, we can make two types of attribution: *internal* and *external*. Internal attributions place the responsibility for behaviour or performance with the individual, whereas external attributions place the reasons in the situation. Consider the following example. A college rugby team has just returned home after their first match, having lost 72–0. They have the unenviable task of explaining the score to others. They make a number of internal or external attributions to explain why they lost so badly. Examples of these attributions are shown in Table 7.1.

Table 7.1 Examples of some internal and external attributions following failure

Internal	External
We are just no good.	The referee was biased.
We didn't try hard enough.	The crowd was on their side.
I let the team down.	They have played together many more times than us.

Table 7.1 shows various attempts to make sense of the catastrophic result. The players adopting the internal attributions are blaming themselves, whereas those adopting the external attributions are blaming other characteristics of the situation. As you can imagine, after a humiliating defeat most of us would tend to adopt external attributions and blame other factors, whereas after a success most of us tend to adopt an internal position and take the credit. This phenomenon is known as self-serving bias.

Whether we make internal or external attributions appears to be related to self-esteem and hence can affect performance. Biddle and Hill (1992) conducted a study in which fifty-eight sixth-form and university students fenced, all for the first time. The outcome of each match was manipulated by the experimenters so that some participants consistently won and others consistently lost. After a series of matches, the attributions and emotional states of the participants were measured. Statistical analysis of the results showed that the attributions made by the students to explain the results were strongly related to the emotions they experienced, particularly in those participants who consistently lost. This shows that in losers, the main predictor of self-esteem is the perception of why they lost.

Weiner's model of attribution

Weiner (1974) produced a model of self-attribution based on two factors: (1) whether an internal or an external attribution is made, and (2) whether this attribution is stable over time or rather varies from one situation to another. The relationship between attribution and stability is shown in Figure 7.3.

Attribution

	Internal	External
Stable	ability	task difficulty
Unstable	effort	luck

Figure 7.3 **Weiner's model of attribution**

If we consistently succeed or fail, our attributions are likely to be stable. This means that we are likely to attribute the outcome to either our ability or the difficulty of the task. Because of self-serving bias, it is more likely that we will attribute success to ability and failure to task difficulty. If our results are less consistent we will probably attribute them to effort or luck. Again, self-serving bias means that we are likely to attribute success to effort and failure to bad luck.

Weiner's model gives us a starting point in working with athletes to correct their attributions. We may wish to shift the attributions of a lazy athlete towards the unstable–internal position so that they realise more effort is needed. We may also wish to shift the attributions of a depressed athlete away from a stable–internal position, so that they cease to blame their lack of ability. This is examined further below, when we look at the idea of learned helplessness. Altering an athlete's attributional state is called reattribution training and is a form of cognitive therapy.

Evaluation of Weiner's model

Weiner's model has given us an excellent starting point for reattribution training. It has also provided a basis for most contemporary research on sporting attribution. Clearly, ability, task difficulty, effort and luck are not the only four possible attributions, although this was never claimed by Weiner. Nonetheless there are some attributions (e.g. to teamwork) that do not neatly fit into his framework.

Learned helplessness and reattribution training

In Chapter 3 we discussed the links between early experiences and attitudes to sport, and concluded that children were not likely to acquire positive attitudes to sport if their early experiences were of failure and humiliation. The same principles can be applied to explain our motivation to continue trying under pressure. Seligman (1975) proposed that if we have negative early experiences in which we consistently fail despite our best efforts, *then we will learn that there is no point in continuing to make those efforts*. Once this has been learned, we will tend to react to any form of adversity by adopting an attitude of helplessness. Although learned helplessness is associated with early experience, it can develop at any time. Even elite athletes can lose their motivation if they meet with successive failures.

Seligman's theory has been applied to several fields in psychology, most notably in the study of the links between childhood experience and depression. With regard to sport, there is an obvious practical application of learned helplessness theory. If athletes can learn to be helpless through experiences of failure, then it follows that, by deliberately exposing them to the experience of success, we should be able to alleviate learned helplessness. Dweck (1975) compared two ways of alleviating learned helplessness in children who were judged to be demotivated by failure. In one condition, children were given a programme of achievable goals that made the experience of success inevitable. In the other reattribution training condition, children were given harder tasks, but when they failed they were taught to blame other factors rather than their own ability. The group who underwent reattributional training improved more in motivation and performance than the programmed success group. This shows that, once learned helplessness has been established, it is not easily alleviated by having more positive experiences. Cognitive interventions such as reattributional training are needed.

Self-efficacy

The term 'self-esteem' has already come up in this chapter, appearing to be important in the link between attributions and performance. Bandura (1982) has introduced the related but distinct concept of self-efficacy. Self-esteem refers to how we *feel* about ourselves. Self-esteem is generally stable across a range of situations. Self-efficacy, by contrast, refers to what we *believe* about our abilities. Unlike self-esteem, self-efficacy is situation-specific. For example, if you are a natural athlete, but have some difficulty in getting to grips with sport psychology, your self-efficacy will probably be considerably greater on the field than in the classroom.

Self-efficacy can exert a powerful effect on performance. As Bandura put it, 'once extraordinary performances are shown to be doable, they become commonplace' (Bandura 1990, p. 29). Bandura proposed that self-efficacy could be boosted by successful performance, verbal persuasion and feedback about performance. Wells *et al.* (1993) set out to test whether self-efficacy could be affected by feedback, and whether changes in self-efficacy could affect performance on a weightlifting task. Students were randomly assigned to three groups. Two of the groups were misled about the weight they were successfully lifting. One group, termed the 'light group', lifted less weight than they believed. A 'heavy group' lifted more than they believed. The third group received accurate information about how much they were lifting. The 'light group', who had received false feedback designed to boost their self-efficacy, were able in a later trial to lift more than they had originally. This finding underlines the importance of giving positive feedback to athletes – even if you exaggerate a little about how well they are doing!

Evaluation of the self-efficacy construct

There is little doubt that self-efficacy is a valid construct. It can be measured, and studies such as Wells *et al.* (1993) have demonstrated that it can be manipulated (as predicted by Bandura) in order to improve performance. As a coach or teacher, self-efficacy is a useful idea to bear in mind during training. It is, however, a less accurate predictor of success than is previous performance. Krane *et al.* (1996) looked at self-efficacy in wrestlers and found that self-efficacy was most important as a predictor of victory when competitors were evenly matched. Like other psychological factors, self-efficacy may make all the difference at very high levels, when competitors are probably physically well-matched.

Contemporary research on motives for sports participation

Although there has been an enormous amount of research into how motivation can be improved in those already participating in sport, rather fewer studies have examined what motivates people to choose to take up sports. Ashford *et al.* (1993) interviewed 336 adults at a community sports centre in Leicester about why they participated in sport and what they enjoyed about it. Four main motivators emerged: physical well-being, psychological well-being, improvement of performance and *assertive achievement* (i.e. to accomplish personal challenges and to gain status). Age and gender significantly affected motivation. Older people were more motivated by psychological well-being than younger people. Men were more motivated by assertive achievement than women. These motives are all intrinsic rather than extrinsic, lending support to the idea that most people come to sport for reasons of intrinsic motivation. Although the four main motivators in the Ashford *et al.* study could be fitted neatly into Maslow's theory, the results did not support Maslow's idea that needs must be satisfied in a certain order.

Of course children's motives for taking part in sport may be different to those of adults. Daley and O'Gara (1998) investigated the motives of 145 children in a British secondary school for taking part in non-compulsory sport, using a questionnaire called the Participation Motivation Inventory (PMI). As in the Ashford *et al.* study, the motives for sports participation differed according to gender and age. Between eleven and fifteen years of age, intrinsic factors became more important and extrinsic factors less so. Girls emerged as more motivated by team-affiliation and achievement than boys.

Summary

Humans have a variety of needs, several of which can be satisfied by the medium of sport. An important distinction is between intrinsic and extrinsic motivation. Contemporary research shows that intrinsic motivation is the more important factor for most participants in sport. Depending on the circumstances, extrinsic motives may increase or act against intrinsic motivation. Maslow has produced a theory of human motivation, which takes a broad approach and attempts to describe the entire range of human motivations. One important motive particularly associated with sport is the need to achieve. The most influential theory seeking to explain achievement came from Atkinson and McClelland, who proposed that we are motivated both by the need to achieve and the need to avoid failure. Two contemporary approaches have emerged as particularly important in working with athletes to improve motivation. Attribution theories are concerned with the ways in which we decide why we performed as we did. By reattribution training, we can help athletes develop healthier attributions, e.g. to attribute failure to effort rather than ability. Self-efficacy is the individual's belief in their abilities. Success, feedback, verbal persuasion and reattribution training can all boost self-efficacy.

1 Describe one theory of human motivation.
2 Describe research findings on why adults choose to participate in sport.
3 Describe one approach to improving an athlete's motivation.

Further reading

Cox R (1998) *Sport psychology, concepts and applications*. Boston, McGraw-Hill. A more detailed account of theories and research into motivation and sport.

Wagner H (1999) *The psychobiology of human motivation*. London and New York, Routledge. A more detailed but highly readable account of physiological approaches to human motivation.

Weinberg R and Gould D (1995) *Foundations of sport and exercise psychology*. Champaign, Human Kinetics. A clear introductory text including a wider range of theories.

8

Skill acquisition

Skills and abilities

Anyone who has participated in any sport at any level will be well aware that they have a certain level of proficiency in that sport. You will also be aware that as you learn a sport, at whatever level, you develop existing and new skills. Each sport requires a different range of skills. Thinking more generally, we all have a set of basic physical abilities, including speed and strength, which underlie our skills. The aim of this chapter is to explore the nature of skills and abilities, and to look at how we might enhance our own sporting skills and those of other athletes. First, it might be helpful to look more closely at precisely what psychologists mean when they use the terms ability and skill.

Definitions

The most commonly accepted definition of a skill comes from Knapp (1963, p. 4): 'the learned ability to bring about pre-determined results with maximum certainty, often with the minimum outlay of time, energy or both.' Thus as we develop a sporting skill, we are aiming to combine speed, power, accuracy and economy of movement, while also minimising the possibility of a catastrophic error. The 'trick' in fulfilling one's potential level of skill is to achieve these ideals simultaneously. Take, for example, the technique of a tennis serve. If a novice or even a moderately skilled player serves with all the speed and power they can muster, the chances are high that they will waste a lot of energy and land the ball outside the target area.

An ability, by contrast, describes our innate (and largely unchangeable) physical attributes that determine our potential for a given sport. Abilities are important because they put limits on the degree of skill we can acquire in a given sport. If you wish to become an elite athlete, it is also a good idea to match up your abilities with an appropriate sport. However good your upper body strength and aerobic fitness, there is little point in cherishing ambitions to be a snooker champion if you have poor manual dexterity and spatial awareness! Table 8.1 shows some motor abilities and the skills that depend on those abilities.

Table 8.1 Examples of motor abilities and skills which depend on these abilities	
motor ability	skills dependent on ability
dynamic strength	power-lift, full-body tackle, bear-hug
reaction time	karate block, sprint start, tennis return
manual dexterity	bowling, basketball manipulation

Classifying abilities

An interesting question for researchers has been the extent to which different physical abilities tend to go together in the same people (the *general motor ability hypothesis*) and the extent to which different athletes have quite different strengths (the *specificity hypothesis*). Most current researchers tend to believe that there is a **superability** factor which has some effect on, but does not directly determine, specific motor abilities. This means essentially that there is a broad tendency for athletes who score highly in one ability to also score highly in others. However, there are many athletes who excel in one or more abilities but not others.

Fleishman (1964) has provided a different way of looking at abilities. He identified two types of motor ability: gross motor abilities and psychomotor abilities. Gross motor abilities are physical attributes such as speed, strength, stamina and flexibility. Psychomotor abilities involve perception as well as physical attributes. An example of a psychomotor ability is reaction time, which requires that we perceive a stimulus, initiate the appropriate response and carry out the motor response. All sports require a blend of gross motor abilities and psychomotor abilities, but some sports have a particular requirement for particular abilities. For example, dynamic strength is particularly important for a weight-lifter, psychomotor abilities less so.

Evaluation of the ability construct

The idea that a set of innate abilities underlie sporting skills has many useful applications, e.g. in choosing those sports in which we might find it easiest to compete seriously. It is also certainly true to say that having certain abilities will make it easier to acquire certain skills. However, we should not take the idea of innate and unchangeable abilities too much to heart. Regular weight training does not merely increase our lifting skills (although it does so), but it also increases our dynamic strength, which in turn allows us to develop further our skills of tackling. In this case the motor ability is certainly not fixed and unchangeable, but can in fact be enhanced by hard training.

Classifying skills

A number of systems for classifying motor skills have been developed in psychology. We can briefly examine some of the most influential distinctions.

Gross and fine skills

The fineness of a motor skill is defined as how much precision is required in the movement. Gross skills are those which require large muscular movement. For example, the major skill involved in the high jump is an upward thrust using the leg muscles. Fine skills require tiny muscular movements, such as are required for an elite standard gymnastic performance. Figure 8.1 shows the continuum of gross to fine motor skills.

Gross ◄───► **Fine**

power-lift   javelin throw   tennis serve   darts throw   ballet pirouette

Figure 8.1 **Examples of sporting skills ranging from gross to fine**

Open and closed skills

The degree to which a motor skill is considered closed is defined by how predictable and unchanging the environment in which it is performed. Sports such as shooting, dance and gymnastics involve highly predictable environments. By contrast ball and contact sports tend to be far less predictable, hence they involve open skills. Picture yourself in the boxing ring facing an opponent. One of the major obstacles you will have to overcome is that you don't know what is coming next. Will, for example, your opponent circle or attack, punch high or low, straight or roundhouse? Dealing with this involves responding to your opponent's plan of attack while formulating and implementing your own at the same time. The skills needed to achieve these goals are open.

Training for open skills may involve using open and closed scenarios. Closed training scenarios are particularly useful when very complex motor skills need to be learned – they would simply be too difficult to learn in an open situation. The martial arts provide a good example of how closed training techniques can be helpful in preparation for open situations. Typically training will involve unvarying sequences of moves, called *kata* or *forms* according to the style. Kata involve entirely closed skills, because the karateka knows precisely what is coming next. However, practitioners of the martial arts involving kata believe that this approach to skill acquisition helps them greatly in open situations.

Figure 8.2 **This martial artist is practising a closed skill, but with sufficient training should be able to use it in an open situation**

Source: Reproduced by kind permission of Chris Balcombe

Discrete, continuous and serial skills

This distinction is based on the extent to which there are clear beginning- and end-points to a movement. Whatever your sport or sports, you probably have to use some discrete skills and some continuous skills.

Discrete skills involve brief actions which have a clear beginning and end. Examples of discrete skills include a goalkeeper's dive, a fielder's throw and a rugby player's drop-kick.

Continuous skills are defined as those which do not have discrete beginnings and ends. They may thus be stopped at any point without the movement being left incomplete. Examples of continuous skills include running and cycling.

Of course much of the time we need to perform a series of different movements in sequence. These skills do not fall neatly into the categories of either discrete or continuous skills. We classify such skills as a third category, called *serial skills*. Serial skills in sport include gymnastic routines and combination punches.

External and internally paced skills

A further system for classifying skills is founded upon the extent to which the timing of the movement is under the control of the athlete. Movements which are largely under the athlete's control are known as internally paced movements. The more an athlete's timing is determined by external events, the more externally paced the skill is said to be. A good example of a skill that is highly internally paced is the cricketer's bowl. The bowler is not constrained by anything else happening on the pitch and has the freedom to choose the pace of the ball. The batsman, by contrast, has to respond to the pace dictated by the bowler. Batting is thus a more externally paced skill.

Think about the following skills:

1   a golf swing
2   a basketball dribble
3   a soccer shoulder-barge
4   a pole-vault

How would you classify them in terms of their openness, discreteness and pacing?

Stages of skill acquisition

Anyone that has ever learned a new sport will be aware that their new skills develop gradually and that they have to concentrate less and less on what they are doing with time. From this starting point, Fitts and Posner (1967) have produced a three-stage model of skill acquisition.

The cognitive stage

In the early stages of trying to acquire a new skill we tend to focus on understanding the nature of the task. We use higher mental processes to analyse what we intend to achieve and how to go about this. The aim of the cognitive stage is to develop a motor programme, i.e. a mental representation of the skill and how to perform it. We use various mental 'tools' to help us with this. We might *discuss* the skill with other learners or more experienced performers. We will make use of our *visual* abilities in several ways at this stage. We watch our limbs closely as we attempt movements. We will probably watch more expert performers. We may also mentally rehearse movements and visualise ourselves performing them correctly. The coach plays an important role in directing visual techniques, e.g. by giving demonstrations and telling us exactly what to look for when observing. Once the cognitive stage is complete we have a motor programme and we can perform the necessary actions to practise the skill.

The associative stage

This is the intermediate stage of acquiring a skill. Once we have developed an effective motor programme, our next task is to practise the skill. With practice, we tend to need to think less and less about the skill in order to perform it successfully. During the associative stage, we rely less on the visual sense and become more dependent on proprioception. Proprioception is the sense by which we feel what is happening to our bodies. In everyday life we use proprioception to be aware of our position and movement. When learning a motor skill, proprioception becomes critical as we learn to *feel* whether our movements are correct without looking. During the associative stage, practice allows us to reduce the frequency of errors and improve our speed, accuracy and consistency.

The autonomous stage

This is achieved when we have mastered the skill to the degree our abilities will permit. By now, performing the skill requires little conscious effort. In fact, thinking about the skill and consciously attempting to improve on it generally *worsens* our performance. Once we can perform the skill without thinking, we are free to concentrate on other things, such as our strategy (individual or team). Fischman and Oxendine (1993) gave the example of Michael Jordan, the elite basketball player, who could dribble the ball at full speed and change direction without any conscious effort, leaving him free to focus on the positions of other players and determine the best strategy to reach the basket.

Evaluation of the three-stage model

The general principle that practice allows us to perform actions automatically and that automatic processing requires little conscious effort is supported by contemporary cognitive psychology (see, for example, Eysenck and Keane 1995). Furthermore, the model is extremely useful to coaches and teachers. Clearly, by understanding what stage a performer has reached, we can provide the optimum balance of demonstration, direct instruction and practice. This becomes particularly important when we suggest that an experienced performer return to the cognitive stage in order to relearn a basic technique (a common occurrence when an athlete changes coach).

On the downside, while the principles underlying the model are sound and while it undoubtedly has useful applications, there is some question as to how *complete* an explanation it provides of skill acquisition. As Fischman and Oxendine (1993) point out, no amount of practice will take an athlete to the autonomous stage if they are not sufficiently motivated. The model also fails to address individual differences in learning style. Some athletes are more dependent on their visual sense, others on proprioception. Some of us are extremely analytical, while others like to 'just do it'. Despite these limitations, however, Fitts and Posner's model remains an influential and useful account of skill acquisition.

Imagine you are coaching in your chosen sport. Devise a training plan for your students incorporating the principles of the Fitts and Posner model.

Progress exercise

The information-processing approach to skills

The information-processing approach in psychology refers to 'the study of cognitive processes by analogy with the computer' (Jarvis 1994, p. 12). Since computers were developed in the 1950s, psychologists have found it useful to look at human mental processes as if they were the operations of a computer. The first psychologist to apply the information-processing approach to skill acquisition was Welford (1968). Like a computer operation, a human skill is seen as having three stages: the input of information (perception), throughput (decision-making) and output (response). A simplified version of Welford's model is shown in Figure 8.3.

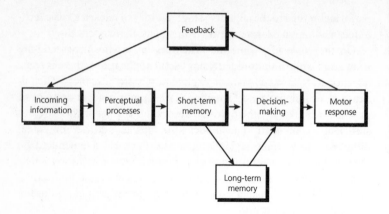

Figure 8.3 **Welford's information-processing model**

The information-processing approach, as exemplified by Welford's model, is useful to sport psychologists because it allows us to break down skills and skill acquisition to their component parts.

Incoming information comes in several forms. Visual information is particularly important in open situations, where we need to be able to respond to what is going on around us. In general, the more closed the skill the less important visual information is. As a bowler in cricket, you would need some visual information to bowl in the right direction, but the last thing you would wish is to be distracted by the crowd. Indeed, athletes who perform very closed routines, such as weight-lifters, frequently report that they have little or no awareness of what is going on around them while performing.

Another important source of incoming information comes from the sense of proprioception. This is important regardless of whether we are practising an open or closed skill. Proprioception allows us to sense our own position and movements. It becomes particularly important when we have mastered a skill. As a skilled performer, we can respond automatically to proprioception without making conscious decisions.

We use the six senses – sight, hearing, taste, smell, touch and proprioception – to receive sensory information. Information enters the information-processing system via all of these senses. In order to avoid being overloaded by this information, we have the ability to selectively attend to important information and filter out irrelevant material. We generally attend to material that we are expecting, that which is particularly relevant to the situation and that which is particularly striking.

Welford conceived short-term memory not just as a store of information but as the point in the information-processing system at which thinking and decision-making occurs, using information from perceptual processes and long-term memory. Decision-making occurs once the necessary information has been processed in short-term memory and signals are sent to the muscles in order to effect the appropriate motor response.

Evaluation of Welford's model

The principle outlined by Welford – that we can break down skills into their components by comparing them to the workings of a computer – remains sound today. In general, the sequence of events outlined by Welford is confirmed by contemporary research. However, more recent research into information processing has revealed some issues not addressed by Welford's approach. The issue of *automatic processing*, for example, is not satisfactorily explained. If a stimulus can be responded to without conscious attention, the model fails to explain at what point in the system it is filtered out from consciousness and what precisely happens to this information. Similarly, the Welford model does not address the factors that put limits on how much information we can process at once and respond to with simultaneous actions.

Memory

The nature of human memory is of interest to sport psychologists, as it is integral to understanding how motor skills are stored and retrieved. Memory is also important because it determines how we learn from experience, bringing information from past experiences to bear on the current situation. A useful information-processing model addressing the general nature of memory comes from Anderson (1983).

Anderson's model of memory

Anderson proposed that there are three functionally separate aspects to memory. Short-term or working memory is where incoming information is processed and conscious thinking and decision-making takes place. Working memory interacts with two separate long-term stores: the procedural store, which comprises our knowledge of motor skills, and the declarative store, which comprises our memory for facts. A simple version of Anderson's model is shown in Figure 8.4.

The declarative store constantly receives information about what is currently occurring. This information is stored for later use. When we need to make a strategic decision, we draw on the information in the declarative store. This might, for example, have information on our strengths and weaknesses and those of the opposition. It might also contain information about alternative strategies we have tried in the past or seen others try. The purpose of the procedural store is quite different. When we learn a new skill we form a mental representation of that skill, what Fitts and Posner called a 'motor programme'. This

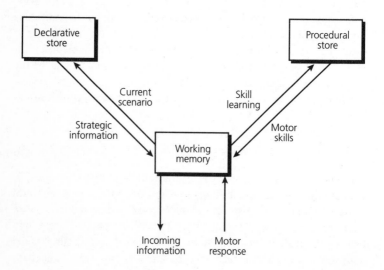

Figure 8.4 Anderson's model of memory

motor programme is kept in the procedural store. When the skill is required, we access the motor programme and retrieve the information necessary to perform the skill.

Evaluation of Anderson's theory

Anderson's theory is quite a good representation of cognitive psychologists' beliefs about the 'functional architecture' of memory. There is considerable evidence for the existence of three separate parts to the memory system. Evidence comes in the main from cases of brain-damaged patients who have lost or partially lost one of the three systems, but have the other two still intact (see, for example, Eysenck and Keyne 1995). The theory explains well how we function in sporting situations. For example, because of the separate mental pathways needed to make strategic decisions (using the declarative store) and to operate motor skills (using the procedural store), you can see that we should be able to perform these two mental tasks simultaneously, *provided* that the motor skill has become automatic, thus not requiring much of the capacity of working memory. In novices, who require working memory to consciously process motor skills, strategic planning cannot be carried out simultaneously.

Theories of motor learning

Whereas Anderson's theory provides us with a good overview of the processes of memory, there are also theories addressing the more specific issue of the storage and retrieval of motor skills. Two theories have emerged as particularly significant: closed loop theory and schema theory.

Closed loop theory

Adams (1971) proposed closed loop theory. This proposes that two separate types of information are stored and that these interact to bring about the motor response. The *memory trace* contains the information needed to initiate the movement or movements. The *perceptual trace* contains the information as to what the movement should *feel like* if it is performed correctly. Once the movement begins, information from the muscles is fed back to the perceptual trace. If it does not match the memory of what the movement *should* feel like, this information is passed on to a central control centre which amends the movement accordingly. This feedback loop is shown in Figure 8.5.

You can see from Figure 8.5 why the theory is called the 'closed loop'. Muscle movement is regulated by a closed feedback loop, involving the two types of stored information.

Evaluation of closed loop theory

The closed loop approach would explain well the familiar experience in which you commence a technique, such as a tennis serve or a golf drive, and immediately become aware that it is not going to be successful. It certainly seems likely that both types of information proposed by Adams are indeed stored. However, as Schmidt (1975) pointed out, some motor responses are simply too quick to involve a feedback loop to perfect the movement. Closed loops are thus not *universal* in motor skills.

Schema theory

Schmidt (1975) proposed schema theory, an alternative approach to that of Adams. A schema is a packet of information, containing all the information we have in relation to one subject. Most cognitive

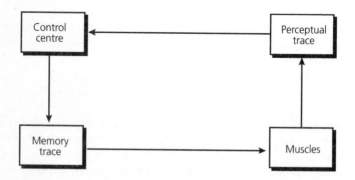

Figure 8.5 **Adams' closed loop theory**

psychologists believe that *knowledge* is stored in schemas. Schmidt went further and proposed that motor skills are stored in schemas as well. Schmidt proposed that when we perform an action we store four types of information. The *initial conditions* include any information about the environment in which the action was performed, the position and state of the body, and the circumstances in which that action was performed. *Certain aspects of the movement*, such as its speed, force and direction are also stored. Schmidt's third type of recorded information concerns the *results of the action*. Clearly if we are to plan, we need to know which actions will have which effects. Finally, we store the *sensory consequences of the action*, i.e. how it felt.

Each action practised will generate two schemas: a *recall schema*, which contains the information needed to reproduce the movement, and a *recognition schema*, which compares the movements generated with those expected, based on past experience of performing the action. Recognition schemas are similar to Adams' perceptual traces. There are two principle differences between schema theory and closed loop theory. First, schema theory does not suggest a feedback loop, thus the recognition schema does not automatically provide feedback to the recall schema. Second, unlike Adams' memory traces, a schema as proposed by Schmidt corresponds to a single movement, not merely a movement in a single situation in a single sport. Thus the skill of sprinting will have a single schema that can be activated in a variety of sporting situations, from track athletics to cricket and rugby.

Evaluation of schema theory

Like closed loop theory, schema theory can explain how we can sense when a move is going awry. The great virtue of schema theory, as opposed to closed loop theory, is its cognitive economy. A general principle of cognitive psychology is that if we could have developed two ways of performing a cognitive process, the chances are that we have evolved the simpler, more efficient system. Because schemas are generalised and can be activated in a variety of situations, they use considerably less processing capacity than perceptual traces, one of which would need to be constructed for every action in every sport. Most contemporary psychologists therefore broadly support schema theory.

Enhancing skill acquisition

You should now have a sound grasp of the psychological principles underlying skill acquisition. The remainder of this chapter is devoted to briefly looking at ways in which these principles can be applied to making sure athletes learn skills effectively. We can apply psychological knowledge to three broad training issues: practice, guidance and feedback.

Practice

It is generally agreed that practice forms an essential part of skill acquisition. As Fitts and Posner (1967) identified in their model of skill acquisition, once the basic technique can be performed (the cognitive stage), the bulk of training will consist of practice (the associative stage). As athlete, coach or teacher, there are various decisions you have to make regarding practice, such as whether it should be massed or distributed, whole or part and physical or mental.

Massed and distributed practice

In *massed practice*, the skill to be mastered is repeated over an extended period. For example, a set of rugby backs might spend a two-hour session just running the line. The alternative to massed practice is *distributed practice*, where practice of the skill to be mastered is interspersed with other training. Massed practice has the advantage that the athlete will probably forget less between practices, but also the disadvantage of leading to boredom. Too much massed practice with a young or inexperienced athlete runs the risk of demotivating them and potentially losing them to the sport.

Whole and part practice

A second issue concerns whether to practise skills in their complete form (whole skill practice) or whether to break them down into their component parts (part skill practice). With *continuous skills*, this is not really an issue – there is little point in practising a single step in running or a single pedal in cycling. However, *serial skills* can sometimes benefit from separate practice of each part. Take, for example, a boxer's combination punches. The combination will not work unless each punch is correct in technique, aim and pace. It is thus well worthwhile to perfect each punch separately. However, if there is too much emphasis on part skill practice there is a risk that the flow of the whole skill may be lost.

Physical and mental practice

It goes without saying that physical skills are enhanced by physical practice. However, an interesting issue concerns the usefulness of *mental* practice, where the athlete visualises themselves performing the skill. In a recent study, Smith *et al.* (1998) asked participants to imagine performing a finger exercise twenty times a day for four weeks. Finger strength improved by an average of 16 per cent. However, mental practice alone is not equivalent to physical practice. In the Smith *et al.* study, participants who *actually performed* the finger exercise increased their strength by 33 per cent. Its generally believed that a combination of physical and mental practice is most useful to athletes, but that physical practice is the more important and should make up the bulk of training.

Guidance

Guidance refers to any information we give learners in order to help them develop their skills. Guidance can be visual, in the form of demonstrations, diagrams, films, etc.; verbal, in the form of instructions; or manual, in the form of physical support or adjustment of posture. These may of course be used in conjunction. An example of this would be guidance to an archer on the correct posture from which to shoot. The coach may begin by demonstrating the stance, then give verbal instructions to improve the learner's position, then finally make tiny adjustments by hand. Demonstration is a good general form of guidance and often a way of beginning a lesson. However, verbal prompts are often needed to improve position and movements. Sometimes verbal instructions are simply too clumsy, and for fine adjustments manual guidance may be needed.

Feedback

Feedback is any information we receive following an action. Feedback is important in skill acquisition because it is knowing how an action we perform compares to our *intended* action that allows us to perfect skills. Feedback can be intrinsic or extrinsic. *Intrinsic feedback* comes directly through our senses. You can, for example, hear when you hit a tennis ball with the frame of the racket. The jarring sensation in your arm will similarly tell you when your golf drive has ploughed straight into the ground! *Extrinsic feedback* comes from others and is a particularly important part of coaching. Extrinsic feedback comes in two forms: knowledge of performance and knowledge of results. *Performance feedback* comes in the form of information about the skill with which we performed an action. *Results feedback* comes in the form of points, goals, times, etc. The effective coach focuses on performance feedback. In the early stages of skill acquisition, before athletes have learned to use proprioception to tell them whether an action was performed correctly, performance feedback is of critical importance.

Summary

When we learn a new sport we acquire proficiency by making use of our general abilities and acquiring specific skills. Skills are central to sporting proficiency. Skills can be classified according to the predictability of the environment, the presence of clear beginning- and end-points to the movement, and the factors that determine the pace at which the action is carried out. Some researchers have proposed distinct stages to the acquisition of skills, beginning with gaining an understanding of the task and progressing with practice. The information-processing approach to psychology allows us to break down skills and analyse them, in the same way as we analyse the functions of a computer. An understanding of memory has also proved useful to understanding skill acquisition. We believe that long-term memory involves two separate stores – one of which, called procedural memory, deals with motor skills. There have been attempts to explain in more detail the nature of procedural memory, including two particularly influential theories: closed loop theory and schema theory. Psychologists have applied their understanding of skill acquisition to the process of coaching, improving our knowledge of practice, guidance and feedback.

Think back to when you learned your main sport. Give a detailed account of the learning process, referring to as many relevant theories as possible. Include details of how your coach applied psychological knowledge to your training.

Review exercise

Further reading

Fischman MG and Oxendine JB (1993) Motor skill learning for effective coaching and guidance. In Williams JM (ed.) *Applied sport psychology, personal growth to peak performance*. Mountain View, Mayfield. A short and readable account of how to apply psychological principles to coaching.

Magill R (1993) *Motor learning: concepts and applications*. Madison, Brown & Benchmark. Covers the areas discussed here in more detail and includes up-to-date theory and research.

9

Study aids

IMPROVING YOUR ESSAY-WRITING SKILLS

At this point in the book you have acquired the knowledge necessary to tackle the exam itself. Answering exam questions is a skill which this chapter shows you how to improve. Examiners have some ideas about what goes wrong in exams. Most importantly, students do not provide the kind of evidence the examiner is looking for. A Grade C answer is typically accurate but has limited detail and commentary, and it is reasonably constructed. To lift such an answer to a Grade A or B may require no more than fuller detail, better use of material and coherent organisation. By studying the essays presented in this chapter, and the examiner's comments, you can learn how to turn Grade C essays into Grade A essays.

Please note that marks given by the examiner in the practice essays should be used as a guide only and are not definitive. They represent the 'raw marks' given by an OCR examiner. That is, the marks the examiner would give to the examining board based on a total of 24 marks per question broken down into Skill A (description) and Skill B (evaluation). They may not be the marks given on the examination certificate received ultimately by the student because all examining boards are required to use a common standardised system called the

Uniform Mark Scale (UMS) which adjusts all raw scores to a single standard acceptable to all examining boards.

The essays are about the length a student would be able to write in 35–40 minutes (leaving you extra time for planning and checking). Each essay is followed by detailed comments about its strengths and weaknesses. The most common problems to look out for are:

- Failure to answer the question set and presenting 'one written during your course'.
- A lack of evaluation or commentary – many weak essays suffer from this.
- Too much evaluation and not enough description. Description is vital in demonstrating your knowledge and understanding of the selected topic.
- Writing 'everything you know' in the hope that something will get credit. Excellence is displayed through selectivity, and therefore improvements can often be made by *removing* material which is irrelevant to the question set.

For more ideas on how to write good essays you should consult *Exam Success in AEB Psychology* (Paul Humphreys) in this series.

Practice essay 1

(a) **Describe what psychologists have discovered about aggression in sport. (8 marks)**
(b) **Evaluate what psychologists have discovered about aggression in sport. (10 marks)**
(c) **Bull (1991) defines aggression, as applied to sport, as 'any behaviour intended to harm another individual or object by physical or verbal means.' Suggest a number of ways in which this type of aggression in sport performers may be controlled. (6 marks)   [OCR 1998]**

Reproduced by permission of the University of Cambridge Local Examination Syndicate.

Candidate's answer

(a) There are different types of behaviour that might appear aggressive in sport. Hostile aggression occurs when a player sets out to maliciously hurt an opponent. Instrumental aggression is when he is still causing hurt, but only to score or save a point, such as when a footballer is about to score. Assertive behaviour looks aggressive but is not aimed at hurting anyone.

Aggression not only appears in sport. A study about aggression by Bandura reflects this. Bandura conducted an experiment to investigate whether aggression was learned or innate. The children used in the experiment were aged between 5 and 9 and were split up into groups. Each group was exposed to either an aggressive or a non aggressive condition. In the non aggressive condition the children played quietly. In the aggressive condition the children were placed in the room with a 5ft Bobo doll, which was being beaten by an adult. The children in this condition imitated the behaviour and attacked the bobo doll. It was concluded from this study that aggression could be considered to be learned from watching others. In relation to sports if a young child watching football sees an action that is aggressive, then because it was on the TV, they could go onto a football pitch and do exactly the same thing.

Aggression can also be because of social pressure. A study by Milgram used adults split up into two groups, a learner and a teacher. The pupil was asked to learn sets of word pairs. When asked to repeat the word pairs, if they gave a wrong answer then the investigator would order the teacher to administer the pupil with an electric shock. Milgram's 'teachers' would give the shocks ie. behave aggressively because there was social pressure on them to do so. This relates to the feeling of players of sport being expected to show some aggression towards opponents, particularly in a grudge match.

Another theory is that all aggression is instinctive, this was called the instinct theory. It suggests that individuals need to show their aggression somehow, to act as a form of catharsis, or cleansing. This could be the reason as to why aggression has not been successfully eliminated in sport. Aggression can be got rid of productively by taking part in sport. If people go into sport in order to get rid of their aggression then it is inevitable that this will sometimes get out of hand. This suggests that sport will make us less aggressive. However,

Arms (1979) found that sport makes spectators more aggressive although it may make players less aggressive, maybe because they are knackered.

Some research has looked at whether aggression makes players more likely to win, particularly in ice hockey, which is a very aggressive sport. Wankel (1973) found that it made no difference. Professional fouls may benefit a team, but getting angry will probably spoil your concentration and lose you the game.

(b) The sample used in the study by Bandura were only small children. This cannot be applied to an everyday situation with adults as children and adults have different views, so that research on children should not be applied to explaining adult aggression. Also, even if people do imitate aggression as children they are often punished. We would then expect aggressive behaviour to be gone by adulthood. It should not then be seen in professional sport.

Milgram's investigation took place under very artificial conditions. It is difficult to compare what went on in a psychology laboratory to what happens on the sportsfield. Also, if we obey authority as Milgram said, we would expect players to respect the referee more and so obey the rules about sporting aggression.

Instinct theory and learning theory may both be partially true in explaining sporting aggression. Instinct theory explains why aggression is so common and hard to get rid of. Learning theory explains how people show aggression and who to.

Wankel only looked at ice hockey which is a very aggressive sport. There should be more research with other sports as we can't apply research from ice hockey to less aggressive sports.

(c) One way of reducing aggression is punishment. If children are punished when they are aggressive as children they may not be so aggressive as adults. This comes from social learning theory. Social learning theory suggests that we can learn by seeing others punished. Therefore people should be made an example of. The media could do this instead of glorifying violence in sport.

According to instinct theory we can let aggression out safely in hard training. Aggressive players could therefore be given extra training. Another way to get rid of aggression is by using a contract. An aggressive player signs a contract promising not to do it again.

This candidate has produced an answer that directly addresses the question and demonstrates a sound understanding. The limiting factor overall is a lack of depth. Part (a), which required description only, begins well with the distinction between different types of aggression. However, this could have been developed further with examples of research into each of the three categories outlined. In the second paragraph the candidate wanders off the point a little, spending considerable time describing research about aggression in general, but they do gain credit for applying the findings to sport. The candidate repeats the same situation in the next paragraph in their description of the Milgram study.

The candidate continues with a description of instinct theory. This is appropriate and leads usefully into a piece of research by Arms *et al.*, although the description of the study is rather oversimple. Incidentally, it is quite acceptable to use theories as well as empirical studies in your answer when a question uses the general term 'research'. Part (a) closes with a brief outline of research into the benefits of aggression to sporting performance. This is useful but once again not developed in sufficient detail.

While Part (a) is a reasonable answer, the candidate falls down somewhat in Part (b). You will notice that Part (b) carries 10 marks, making it the most important section. This candidate has committed the classic error of writing least for the section carrying the most marks. Some good points are made, but again there are missed opportunities to expand on points and to focus on research specific to sport as opposed to more general research.

Part (c) is brief but well-focused on the question. Social learning theory and instinct theory are applied to the question, and contracting is introduced. Again the candidate misses out on the high marks by failing to go beyond the most basic introduction to the approaches they have chosen.

In conclusion this is a no-frills answer that focuses on the question and demonstrates some knowledge of sport psychology research and the ability to apply more general psychological research to sport. However, the candidate's knowledge of sport psychology research appears to be quite limited, and they miss numerous opportunities to expand on ideas. Part (b) is particularly weak. This essay scored a total of 10/24, a borderline pass. To raise it to a higher grade, the candidate would have to demonstrate greater knowledge of research into aggression in sport, and in particular more critical awareness of this research.

Practice essay 2

(a) **Describe what psychologists have learned about the effects of an audience on human performers. (8 marks)**

(b) **Evaluate what psychologists have found out about the effects of an audience on human performers. (10 marks)**

(c) **Suggest reasons why teams often have an advantage when 'playing at home'. (6 marks)** [OCR 1998]

Reproduced by permission of the University of Cambridge Local Examination Syndicate.

Candidate's answer

(a) There are numerous pieces of research based upon the effects of an audience on human performers. The first piece of research was designed by Triplett.

Triplett noticed that when looking at cycling records paced times were faster than unpaced times and competitive times were fastest of all. Triplett set up a controlled experiment to determine why this happened. To do this he watched young children winding a fishing reel either alone or in pairs. The results showed that the children wound the reel faster in pairs. He put this down to 'dynamogy' asserting that an audience or coactors increases arousal and ultimately increases the speed in which an act takes place.

The second piece of research was designed by Martens. Martens aimed to see what effects an audience has on learning and performing. To measure this he used male students to carry out a relatively complex task which took practice until it was successful. This task was either carried out alone or with an audience of ten other males. To measure this Martens used the Palmer sweat index. The results showed that during both practice and performance the arousal levels were highest when the audience was present. However, during the practice the students learned more when alone, yet during the performance the students performed better when an audience was present. Therefore the presence of an audience can be advantageous and detrimental.

The final piece of research was developed by Zajonc. Zajonc developed a theory which demonstrates the effect of an audience being present. This theory was based on Hull's drive theory. It is based on 4 tenets. Firstly the presence of an audience increases arousal, secondly early in learning or for simple tasks the dominant response is the correct response; thirdly late in learning or for complex tasks the dominant response is the incorrect response; and finally the immediate response to act is the dominant response.

These three pieces of research therefore show that the presence of an audience can be both beneficial and detrimental. However this depends on whether the subject is learning or performing the task. Also an increase in arousal can determine an increase in speed according to Triplett's concept of 'dynamogeny.'

(b) These pieces of research can be evaluated in a number of ways. Firstly the subject sample used in both Triplett's and Martens' study are weak. This is firstly because in Triplett's study only children are used in the task of winding a reel. This is not representative of society in general, as society is made up of adults as well as children, Similarly in Martens' study only male students were used. This is also not representative of society. Therefore both methods used can not be made generalisable to the rest of society.

Secondly, the methodology can be critically evaluated. Firstly in Triplett's study, a controlled experiment was used. Therefore the variables were controlled. This quite a reliable method as it ensures that each time the test was carried out in a similar way each time. In contrast, in Martens' study, the only way arousal was measured was by using the Palmer sweat index. Using this method does not allow for other conditions such as the feelings of the individual to be taken into consideration. For example the emotions of the student may have resulted in a higher arousal level compared to what they usually would have. This may render the results unreliable.

The final evaluative point is that of usefulness. All of these pieces of research have useful elements which could be taken on board by others. Firstly in Martens' research, he suggests that during the learning stage of an act, the individual is more likely to benefit from doing it alone, whereas during the performance they will benefit from an audience. This may prove useful to a beginner who has just started a sport or activity. Similarly, in Triplett's study he suggested that an audience can increase arousal and ultimately the speed of an activity. This may prove useful in sports where speed is an important element. This is reinforced by Hull, as he suggests that an audience can benefit those performing a simple or well-learned task.

(c) There are numerous reasons why teams often have an advantage. This may firstly be because teams are aware that there may be people they know in the audience and this may increase their arousal levels. According to Triplett this is beneficial because it can increase speed (dynamogeny concept) which can be an advantage when playing a sport such as cricket.

Another possible reason why teams have an advantage at home may be because they are knowledgeable of the surroundings, therefore they can exert their energy into playing their sport, as opposed to having to get used to a different surrounding. This may allow the team to focus on the game. In relation to Martens' study this may be because the team have learned well to play at home, this improving their performance. In contrast if a team is not playing, they have to learn to play on a different pitch and ultimately their performance could be affected.

Examiner's comments

This candidate has done a very good job of directly addressing the question. The principal difference between this answer and the last is that this candidate has displayed a good general knowledge of research findings and theory in sport psychology. The essay is well structured. Each part to the question is quickly and efficiently introduced, and it is generally made quite clear how each theory, study and evaluation point relates to the question.

In Part (a) an appropriate selection of two pieces of research and a theory are described. It is, incidentally, quite acceptable to describe both theory and research in answering a question of this type, even if the question uses the term 'research'. The limiting factor in gaining marks was precision of description. Neither Martens' study nor Zajonc's theory is described sufficiently clearly for a reader unfamiliar with the area to grasp quite what took place.

In Part (b) the candidate has sensibly approached the task by addressing both the methodological weaknesses of studies and the usefulness of the applications derived from the research. A common shortcoming in essays is to focus just on criticisms and not look for the positive. The candidate displayed a good knowledge of the methodological details of the research, as well as critical awareness. This was pleasing to see. For maximum marks, the candidate would be required to display further knowledge, either by expanding on existing points or raising further issues.

In Part (c) the candidate has raised and briefly explored two valid reasons why home teams may have an advantage. The limiting factor here is the depth to which the link between audiences and arousal has been explored – there is considerably more that could be said.

In conclusion, this candidate has attacked the question directly and appropriately, displaying a sound knowledge of research in sport psychology and good critical awareness. The total mark was 19/24, Grade B. The only limiting factor in this candidate's mark is the depth to which some issues are explored. To attain a Grade A, slightly more detail is needed, particularly in Part (c).

KEY RESEARCH SUMMARY

Article 1

'An analysis of the relationship between hostility and training in the martial arts', Kevin Daniels and Everard W. Thornton in *Journal of Sport Sciences* (1990) 8, 95–101

Article notes

This is a study of hostile behaviour in martial artists, conducted at Liverpool University. There are a number of methodological issues you may wish to consider when evaluating this study. The participants were sampled from university sports clubs. They may thus not be a representative sample of martial artists and other athletes as a whole. It is also worth bearing in mind that hostility was assessed by a self-report questionnaire. This requires a degree of honesty and self-awareness. A further limitation lies in the fact that sample sizes were quite small, thus personality differences in participants might have affected results. The authors were aware of the limitations of the study and expressed the need for further research in this area. Despite its limitations, the study is useful in confirming what martial artists generally report: their training reduces rather than increases their aggression. This summary omits some complex methodological and statistical details.

Summary

Introduction Anecdotal accounts of the effects of martial arts training on aggression have arrived at conflicting conclusions. While martial artists generally claim reduced aggression, critics have observed the opposite. Different theories of aggression would also predict different outcomes. While instinct theories and the frustration–aggression hypothesis would suggest that combative sport should reduce aggression through catharsis, social learning theory would suggest that combative sport involves the exposure to aggressive models and the learning of a violent repertoire of behaviour, thus leading to increased aggression. Daniels and Thornton (1990) set out to test how martial artists compared with participants in other sports in their levels of hostility. They also aimed to establish whether length of martial arts training appeared to increase or decrease hostility.

Method Five groups of eighteen participants were selected from students of Liverpool University. Group 1 were members of the karate club, Group 2 from the jiu-jitsu club, Group 3 from the rugby club, Group 4 from the badminton club and Group 5 from students who did not participate in university sports. The use of these five groups allowed researchers to compare martial artists with participants in another contact sport, a non-contact sport and non-athletes.

The hostility of each group was assessed using a modernised version of a traditional measure of hostility, the Buss–Durkee Hostility Inventory, developed in 1957. The customised hostility test comprised thirty-two questions which set out to measure three types of hostility: assaultive (violent), indirect (tantrums and destruction of inanimate objects) and verbal. Groups 1–4 filled in the test at training sessions, Group 5 in their rooms.

Results   No overall differences were found between the hostility of the five groups. Interestingly, however, martial artists just beginning training reported higher levels of hostility than other athletes, whereas more experienced martial artists reported lower levels of hostility. Looking in more detail at the subscales of the Buss–Durkee Hostility Inventory, assaultive hostility declined significantly with martial arts training, whereas indirect hostility increased slightly (although this effect was not statistically significant).

Conclusions   Overall, the study supports the idea that martial arts training decreases physical aggression. Certainly respondents appeared to be less likely to resort to violence towards people, although a cautionary note is sounded by the findings that indirect hostility increased. Although this was not statistically significant in this study, significant results have been found in previous studies, e.g. Rothpearl (1980).

Glossary

The first occurrence of each of these terms is highlighted in **bold** type in the main text. An asterisk has been used to indicate that a word or phrase has an entry of its own in this glossary.

academic sport psychology A broad field, including all aspects of the psychology of sport.

anxiety Negative emotional state of worry and apprehension, combined with heightened arousal*.

applied sport psychology A narrower field than sport psychology, focused purely on ways to improve athletic performance.

arousal The body's degree of activation, regulated by hormone levels which are in turn regulated by the brain.

assaultive hostility Hostility involving physical violence.

assertiveness Apparently aggressive behaviour that is unlikely to cause harm to another person.

attribution The mental process whereby we 'attribute' causes to events.

behavioural psychology Psychology deriving from the behaviourist tradition, which emphasises observable behaviour and the importance of learning.

catharsis The process of 'letting out' a built-up emotion such as anger or grief.

cognitive anxiety The psychological experience of anxiety*, including thoughts of losing, humiliation and personal inadequacy.

cognitive dissonance The sensation we experience when we encounter new information that is not compatible with an attitude we currently hold.

cognitive–behavioural techniques A range of psychological interventions based upon altering an individual's patterns of thinking, e.g. to make them more confident.

collectivist culture A culture in which, in contrast to an individualist culture*, people identify themselves primarily as part of groups and only secondarily as individuals.

desensitise To become used to a stimulus so that it no longer triggers the same reaction.

ethology The study of animal behaviour.

factor analysis A mathematical technique designed to show which variables in a population cluster in the same individuals.

frustration–aggression hypothesis The notion that aggression is caused by frustration and frustration leads to aggression.

functional approach (to attitudes) An approach which looks at how attitudes are useful to us.

groupthink The phenomenon whereby group cohesion is so strong that individuals are prevented from contradicting the majority view.

hostile aggression Aggression where the main intention is to cause harm to another person.

imagery The use of the 'mind's eye' in a range of psychological techniques designed to induce relaxation and increased confidence.

individualist culture A culture in which, in contrast to a collectivist culture*, people identify themselves primarily as individuals and secondarily as group members.

instinct An in-born tendency towards a behaviour.

instrumental aggression Aggression where the main intention is to achieve an aim and the fact that injury is likely to be caused is incidental.

narrow-band theory An approach to personality which focuses on one specific aspect of behaviour.

natural selection The evolutionary process whereby those individuals best adapted to their environment survive and pass on the genes for those characteristics.

observational learning Acquiring behaviour by observing it displayed in others.

operant conditioning Learning that is contingent on reinforcement of a behaviour.

outcome goal A goal based on achieving a certain level of competitive success, e.g. winning contests or getting to a certain position in a league.

paratelic state A metamotivational state in which the person seeks high arousal*.

performance goal A goal based on selecting and improving on a particular aspect of performance.

personality profiling An approach to personality testing which involves assessing the individual on a range of measures.

psychological contract An agreement, e.g. between coach and athlete, in which the athlete agrees to modify their behaviour.

role model An individual whose behaviour is observed and imitated.

sanctioned aggression Aggression that is officially or unofficially accepted by parties in sport.

self-rating inventory A test of personality in which the participant responds to a number of questions or statements.

sensation seeking The amount of stimulation an individual requires to reach their preferred level of arousal*.

social learning theory A theory of development which sees behaviour as being learned by imitation and reinforcement.

social loafing The phenomenon whereby individuals operating in a team each contribute less to the team effort than they would if operating alone.

somatic anxiety The bodily experience of anxiety*, including physical symptoms such as increased heart rate and blood pressure.

sphygmomanometer An apparatus for measuring blood pressure.

state anxiety The state of anxiety* experienced before and during competition.

stereotypes Beliefs that exaggerate similarities and minimise differences between members of a group.

stress The entire process whereby an individual perceives a threat and responds with physiological and psychological changes including increased arousal* and anxiety*.

structural approach (to attitudes) An approach which looks at the components that make up an attitude.

superability A broad general tendency for a certain level of attainment across a range of different abilities.

survival trait A characteristic that makes the individual better adapted to their environment.

team-building Process of using psychological techniques to increase group cohesion in a team.

telic dominance The extent to which an individual is dominated by telic states, i.e. seeking low arousal*.

trait anxiety The individual's tendency towards anxiety*, regardless of situation.

trait theories A group of theories of personality which share the assumptions that personality is measurable and consists of discrete characteristics or traits.

vicarious reinforcement Reinforcement that is obtained from observing the consequences of behaviour in others.

Bibliography

Adams JA (1971) A closed loop theory of motor learning. *Journal of motor behaviour* 3, 111–50.

Ajzen I and Fishbein M (1980) *Understanding attitudes and predicting social behaviour*. Englewood Cliffs, Prentice Hall.

Anderson JR (1983) *The architecture of cognition*. Harvard, Harvard University Press.

Anshell MH (1992) The case against the certification of sport psychologists: in search of the phantom expert. *The sport psychologist* 6, 265–86.

Apter MJ (1993) Phenomenological frames and the paradoxes of experience. In Kerr JH, Murgatroyd S and Apter MJ (eds) *Advances in reversal theory*. Amsterdam, Swets & Zeitlinger.

Apter MJ (1997) Reversal theory, what is it? *The psychologist*, May, 217–20.

Arms RL, Russell GW and Sandilands ML (1979) Effects of viewing aggressive sports on the hostility of spectators. *Social psychology quarterly* 42, 275–9.

Aronson E, Wilson TD and Akert RM (1994) *Social Psychology*. New York, Harper Collins.

Ashford B, Biddle S and Goudas M (1993) Participation in community sport centres: motives and predictors of enjoyment. *Journal of sport sciences* 11, 249–56.

Asken MJ (1991) The challenge of the physically challenged: delivering sport psychology services to physically disabled athletes. *The sport psychologist* 5, 370–81.

Bakker FC, Whiting HTA and Van Der Brug H (1990) *Sport psychology: concepts and applications*. Chichester, Wiley.

Bandura A (1965) Influence of models' reinforcement contingencies on the acquisition of imitative responses. *Journal of personality and social psychology* 1, 589, 595.

Bandura A (1973) *Aggression: a social learning analysis*. Englewood Cliffs, Prentice Hall.

Bandura A (1977) *Social learning theory*. Englewood Cliffs, Prentice Hall.

Bandura A (1982) Self-efficacy mechanism in human agency. *American psychologist* 37, 122–47.

Bandura A (1990) Perceived self-efficacy in the exercise of personal agency. *Journal of applied sport psychology* 2, 128–63.

Baron A (1977) *Human aggression*. New York, Plenum.

Baron A and Byrne D (1994) *Social psychology: understanding human interaction*. Boston, Allyn & Bacon.

Baron RA and Richardson DR (1992) *Human aggression*. New York, Plenum.

Bell GJ and Howe BL (1988) Mood state profiles and motivations of triathletes. *Journal of sport behaviour* 11, 66–77.

Bem DJ (1967) Self-perception: an alternative interpretation of cognitive dissonance phenomena. *Psychological Review* 74, 183–200.

Berkowitz L (1993) *Aggression: its causes, consequences and control*. Philadelphia, Temple University Press.

Biddle S and Hill AB (1992) Relationships between attributions and emotions in a laboratory-based sporting contest. *Journal of sport sciences* 10, 65–75.

Bowers KS (1973) Situationalism in psychology: an analysis and a critique. *Psychological review* 80, 307–36.

Carron AV (1993) The sport team as an effective group. In Williams JM (ed.) *Applied sport psychology, personal growth to peak performance*. Mountain View, Mayfield.

Carron AV, Spink KS and Prapavessis H (1997) Team-building and cohesiveness in the sport and exercise setting: use of interventions. *Journal of applied sport psychology* 9, 61–72.

Cattell RB (1965) *The scientific analysis of personality*. Baltimore, Penguin.

Chirivella EC and Martinez LM (1994) The sensation of risk and motivational tendencies in sports: an empirical study. *Personality and individual differences* 16, 777–86.

Clingman JM and Hilliard DV (1987) Some personality characteristics of the super-adherer: following those who go beyond fitness. *Journal of sport behaviour* 10, 123–36.

Collins D (1998) 'In the event': how does anxiety affect performance? *Proceedings of the 1998 BPS conference* 6(2), 104.

Cottrell NB (1968) Performance in the presence of other human beings: mere presence, audience and affiliation effects. In Simmel EC, Hoppe RA and Milton GA (eds) *Social facilitation and imitative behaviour*. Boston, Allyn & Bacon.

Cox R (1998) *Sport psychology, concepts and applications*. Boston, McGraw-Hill.

Daley A and O'Gara A (1998) Age, gender and motivation for participation in extra-curricular physical activities in secondary school adolescents. *European physical education review* 4(1), 47–53.

Daniels K and Thornton E (1990) An analysis of the relationship between hostility and training in the martial arts. *Journal of sport sciences* 8, 95–101.

Danish SJ (1996) Learning life skills through sports. *APA monitor* 9, 9.

Davis H (1991) Criterion validity of the athletic motivation inventory: issues in professional sport. *Journal of applied sport psychology* 3, 176–82.

Dollard J, Miller N, Doob I, Mourer OH and Sears RR (1939) *Frustration and aggression*. New Haven, Yale University Press.

Drewe SB (1998) Competing conceptions of competition: implications for physical education. *European physical education review* 4(1), 5–20.

Durkin K (1995) *Social developmental psychology*. London, Blackwell.

Dweck CS (1975) The role of expectations and attributions in alleviating learned helplessness. *Journal of personality and social psychology* 31, 674–85.

European Federation of Sport Psychology (1996) Position statement of the FEPSAC: 1. Definition of sport psychology. *The sport psychologist* 10, 221–3.

Eysenck HJ (1952) *The scientific study of personality*. London, Routledge & Kegan Paul.

Eysenck HJ (1966) *Fact and fiction in psychology*. Baltimore, Penguin.

Eysenck HJ (1975) *The inequality of man*. San Diego, Edits Publishers.

Eysenck HJ, Nias DKB and Cox DN (1982) Sport and personality. *Advances in behavioural research and therapy* 4(1), 1–56.

Eysenck M and Keane M (1995) *Cognitive psychology*. Hove, LEA.

Fazey J and Hardy L (1988) *The inverted U hypothesis: a catastrophe for sport psychology?* British Association of Sport Sciences Monograph 1. Leeds, National Coaching Foundation.

Festinger LA (1957) *A theory of cognitive dissonance*. New York, Harper Collins.

Festinger LA, Schachter S and Back K (1950) *Social pressures in informal groups: a study of human factors in housing*. New York, Harper & Bros.

Fiedler F (1967) *A theory of leadership effectiveness*. New York, McGraw-Hill.

Fischman MG and Oxendine JB (1993) Motor skill learning for effective coaching and performance. In Williams JM (ed.) *Applied sport psychology, personal growth to peak performance*. Mountain View, Mayfield.

Fitts PM and Posner MI (1967) *Human performance*. Belmont, Brooks/Cole.

Fleishman EA (1964) *The structure and measurement of physical fitness*. Englewood Cliffs, Prentice Hall.

Fortier MS, Vallerand RJ, Briere NM and Provencher PJ (1995) Competitive and recreational sport structures and gender: a test of their relationship with sport motivation. *International journal of sport psychology* 26, 24–39.

Freud S (1919) *Lines of advance in psychoanalytic therapy*. London, Hogarth.

Garland DJ and Barry JR (1990) Personality and leader behaviors in collegiate football: a multidimensional approach to performance. *Journal of research in personality* 24, 355–70.

Gervis M (1991) Children in sport. In Bull S (ed.) *Sport psychology, a self-help guide*. Marlborough, Crowood.

Gill DL (1986) *Psychological dynamics of sport*. Champaign, Human Kinetics.

Gill DL (1994) A sport and exercise psychology perspective on stress. *Quest* 46, 20–7.

Gould D and Krane V (1992) The arousal–performance relationship: current status and future directions. In Horn TS (ed.) *Advances in sport psychology*. Champaign, Human Kinetics.

Gross R (1996) *Psychology, the science of mind and behaviour.* London, Hodder & Stoughton.

Grouios G (1992) Mental practice: a review. *Journal of sport behaviour* 15, 42–59.

Hagger M, Cale L and Almond L (1997) Children's physical activity levels and attitudes towards physical activity. *European physical education review* 3(2), 144–64.

Hanin Y (1986) State–trait anxiety research on sports in the USSR. In Spielberger C and Dias-Guerrero R (eds) *Cross-cultural anxiety.* Washington, Hemisphere.

Hardy L (1996) Testing the predictions of the cusp catastrophe model of anxiety and performance. *The sport psychologist* 10, 140–56.

Hardy L, Parfitt G and Pates J (1994) Performance catastrophes in sport: a test of the hysteresis hypothesis. *Journal of sport sciences* 12, 327–34.

Harris DV and Williams JM (1993) Relaxation and energising techniques for regulation of arousal. In Williams JM (ed.) *Applied sport psychology, personal growth to peak performance.* Mountain View, Mayfield.

Horner MS (1972) Towards an understanding of achievement-related conflicts in women. *Journal of social issues* 28(2), 157–75.

Hull CL (1943) *Principles of behaviour.* New York, Appleton-Century-Crofts.

Husman BF and Silva JM (1984) Aggression in sport: definitional and theoretical considerations. In Silver JM and Weinberg RS (eds) *Psychological foundations of sport.* Champaign, Human Kinetics.

Inlay GJ, Carda RG, Stanborough ME, Dreiling AM and O'Connor PJ (1995) Anxiety and performance: a test of zone of optimal functioning theory. *International journal of sport psychology* 26, 295–306.

Jacobsen E (1929) *Progressive relaxation.* Chicago, University of Chicago Press.

Janis IL (1982) *Victims of groupthink.* Boston, Houghton Mifflin.

Jarvis M (1994) Attention and the information-processing approach. *Psychology teaching* 3, 12–22.

Johnson S, Ostrow AC, Perna FM and Etzel EF (1997) The effects of group versus individual goal-setting on bowling performance. *The sport psychologist* 11, 190–200.

Jones G (1991) Recent developments and current issues in competitive state anxiety research. *The psychologist* 4, 152–5.

Jones G, Swain A and Hardy L (1993) Intensity and direction dimensions of competitive state anxiety and relationships with performance. *Journal of sport sciences* 11, 525–32.

Kenyon GS (1968) Six scales for assessing attitudes towards physical activity. *Research quarterly* 39, 566–74.

Kerr JH (1997) *Motivation and emotion in sport*. London, Taylor & Francis.

Kirkpatrick SA and Locke EA (1991) Leadership: do traits matter? *Academy of management executive* 5(2), 48–60.

Knapp B (1963) *Skills in sport*. London, Routledge & Kegan Paul.

Krane TD, Marex MA, Zaccaro SJ and Blair Z (1996) Self-efficacy, personal goals and wrestlers' self-regulation. *Journal of sport and exercise psychology* 18, 36–48.

Krane V (1998a) Lesbians in sport. *Proceedings of the 1998 BPS annual conference* 6(2), 109.

Krane V (1998b) Sport: experiences in diversity or diverse experiences. *Proceedings of the 1998 BPS annual conference* 6(2), 109.

Kremer J and Scully D (1994) *Psychology in sport*. London, Taylor & Francis.

Leith L (1991) Aggression. In Bull S (ed.) *Sport psychology, a self-help guide*. Marlborough, Crowood.

Lerner BS and Locke EA (1995) The effects of goal-setting, self-efficacy, competition and personality traits on the performance of an endurance task. *Journal of sport and exercise psychology* 17, 138–52.

Lewin K, Lippitt R and White RR (1939) Patterns of aggressive behaviour in experimentally created social climates. *Journal of social psychology* 10, 271–99.

Likert RA (1932) A technique for the measurement of attitudes. *Archives of psychology* 140, 1–55.

Locke EA and Latham GP (1985) The application of goal-setting to sports. *Journal of sport psychology* 7, 205–22.

Lore RK and Schultz LA (1993) Control of human aggression. *American psychologist* 48, 16–25.

Lorenz K (1966) *On aggression*. New York, Harcourt, Brace & World.

Magill R (1993) *Motor learning: concepts and applications*. Madison, Brown & Benchmark.

Maslow A (1954) *Personality and motivation*. New York, Harper Collins.

Martens RA (1977) *Sport competition anxiety*. Champaign, Human Kinetics.

Martens R, Burton D, Vealey RS, Bump LA and Smith D (1990) Development and validation of the competitive state anxiety inventory-2. In Martens R, Vealey RS and Burton D (eds) *Competitive anxiety in sport*. Champaign, Human Kinetics.

McCarthy JF and Kelly BR (1978) Aggressive behaviour and its effects on performance over time in ice hockey athletes: an archival study. *International journal of sport psychology* 9, 90–6.

McClelland DC, Atkinson JW, Clark RW and Lowell EJ (1953) *The achievement motive*. New York, Appleton-Century-Crofts.

McGill JC, Hall JR, Ratliff WR and Moss RF (1986) Personality characteristics of professional rodeo cowboys. *Journal of sport behaviour* 9, 143–51.

McNair DM, Lorr M and Droppelman LF (1972) *Profile of mood states manual*. San Diego, Educational and Industrial Testing Service.

Michaels JW, Blommel JM, Brocato RM, Linkous RA and Rowe JS (1982) Social facilitation and inhibition in a natural setting. *Replications in social psychology* 2, 21–4.

Miller Brewing Company (1983) *The Miller Lite report on American attitudes towards sports*. Milwaukee: Author.

Mischel W (1968) *Personality and adjustment*. New York, Wiley.

Mischel W (1990) *Introduction to personality*. New York, Holt, Rhinehart & Winston.

Moorhead G and Griffin RW (1998) *Organizational behaviour*. Boston, Houghton Mifflin.

Morgan WP (1979) Prediction of performance in athletics. In Klavora P and Daniels JV (eds) *Coach, athlete and sport psychologist*, Champaign, Human Kinetics.

Morgan WP and Goldston SE (1987) Summary. In Morgan WP and Goldston SE (eds) *Exercise and mental health*. Washington, Hemisphere.

Morgan WP, O'Connor PJ, Ellickson KA and Bradley PW (1988) Personality structure, mood states and performance in elite male distance runners. *International journal of sport psychology* 19, 247–63.

Mullins J (1993) Victory in sight. *New scientist* supplement, October, 4–9.

Murgatroyd S, Rushton C, Apter MJ and Ray C (1978) The development of the telic dominance scale. *Journal of personality assessment* 12, 519–28.

Nevill AM and Cann GJ (1998) Does home advantage peak with crowd sizes? *Proceedings of the 1998 BPS annual conference* 6(2), 112.

Nicklaus J (1974) *Golf my way*. New York, Simon & Schuster.

Nosanchuk TA (1981) The way of the warrior. The effects of traditional martial arts training on aggressiveness. *Human relations* 34, 435–44.

Oppenheim AN (1992) *Questionnaire design, interviewing and attitude measurement*. London, Pinter.

Osgood CE, Suki CJ and Tannenbaum PH (1957) *The measurement of meaning*. Urbana, University of Illinois Press.

Pennington D (1986) *Essential social psychology*. London, Edward Arnold.

Pervin L (1993) *Personality theory and research*. New York, Wiley.

Petruzello SJ, Landers FJ and Salazar W (1991) Biofeedback and sports/exercise performance: applications and limitations. *Behaviour therapy* 22, 379–92.

Phillips DP (1986) Natural experiments on the effects of mass-media violence on fatal aggression: strengths and weaknesses of a new approach. In Berkowitz L (ed.) *Advances in experimental social psychology*. Orlando, Academic Press.

Prapavessis H and Grove JR (1991) Precompetitive emotions and shooting performance: the mental health and zones of optimal function models. *The sport psychologist* 5, 223–34.

Randle S and Weinberg R (1997) Multidimensional anxiety and performance: an exploratory examination of the zone of optimal functioning hypothesis. *The sport psychologist* 11, 160–74.

Richards B (1994) The glory of the game. In Richards B (ed.) *Disciplines of delight*. London, Free Association.

Rothpearl AB (1980) Personality traits in the martial arts: a descriptive approach. *Perceptual and motor skills* 50, 395–401.

Russell GW (1993) *The social psychology of sport*. New York, Springer-Verlag.

Saul H (1993) Dying swans? *Scientific American* December, 25–7.

Schmidt RA (1975) A schema theory of discrete motor skill learning. *Psychological review* 82, 225–60.

Schurr KT, Ashley MA and Joy KL (1977) A multivariate analysis of male athlete characteristics: sport type and success. *Multivariate experimental clinical research* 3, 53–68.

Searle A (1996) Group psychology, valuable lessons from our 'newfangled' subject. *Psychology review* 2(3), 34.

Seligman MEP (1975) *Helplessness on depression, development and death*. San Francisco, Freeman.

Sidney KH, Niinimaa V and Shephard RJ (1983) Attitudes towards exercise and sports: sex and age differences, and changes with endurance training. *Journal of sport sciences* 1, 195–210.

Simon J and Smoll FL (1974) An instrument for assessing children's attitudes towards physical activity. *Research quarterly* 45, 407–15.

Slater MR and Sewell DF (1994) An examination of the cohesion–performance relationship in university hockey teams. *Journal of sport sciences* 12, 423–31.

Smith MB, Bruner JS and White RW (1964) *Opinions and personality*. New York, Wiley.

Smith D, Holmes P, Collins D and Layland K (1998) The effect of mental practice on muscle strength and EMG activity. *Proceedings of the British Psychological Society annual conference* 6(2), 116.

Spielberger CD (1966) *Anxiety and behaviour*. New York, Academic Press.

Sutton J (1994) Aggression and violence. In McKnight J and Sutton J (eds) *Social psychology*. Sydney, Prentice Hall.

Swain A and Jones G (1993) Intensity and frequency dimensions of competitive state anxiety. *Journal of sport sciences* 11, 533–42.

Tenenbaum G, Stewart E and Singer RN (1997) Aggression and violence in sport: an ISSP position stand. *The sport psychologist* 11, 1–7.

Terry P (1991) The psychology of the coach–athlete relationship. In Bull S (ed.) *Sport psychology, a self-help guide*. Marlborough, Crowood.

Theodorakis Y (1992) Prediction of athletic participation: a test of planned behaviour theory. *Psychology and motor skills* 74, 371–9.

Thirer J (1993) *Aggression*. In Singer RN, Murphey M and Tennant LK (eds) *Handbook of research on sport psychology*. New York, Macmillan.

Thurstone LL and Chave EJ (1929) *The measurement of attitudes*. Chicago, University of Chicago Press.

Tomes C and Morley A (1998) Spectator aggression in sports fans: an exploration of this and why it differs. *Proceedings of the 1998 BPS annual conference* 6(2), 117.

Triandis HC (1991) Cross-cultural differences in assertiveness/competition vs group loyalty/cooperation. In Hinde RA and Groebels J (eds) *Cooperation in social behaviour*. Cambridge, Cambridge University Press.

Triplett N (1898) The dynamogenic factors in pacemaking and competition. *American journal of psychology* 9, 507–53.

Tuckman BW and Jensen MA (1977) Stages of small group development revisited. *Group and organisational studies* 2, 419–27.

Tutko TA and Ogilvie BC (1966) *Athletic motivation inventory*. San Jose, Institute for the Study of Athletic Motivation.

Vealey RS (1989) Sport personology: a paradigmatic and methodological analysis. *Journal of sport and exercise psychology* 11, 216–35.

Vealey RS and Walter SM (1993) Imagery training for performance enhancement and personal development. In Williams JM (ed.) *Applied sport psychology, personal growth to peak performance*. Mountain View, Mayfield.

Wagner H (1999) *The psychobiology of human motivation*. London and New York, Routledge.

Waller NG, Koietin BA, Bouchard TJ, Lykken DT and Tellegan A (1990) Genetic and environmental influences on religious interests, attitudes and values: a study of twins reared apart and together. *Psychological science* 1, 138–42.

Wankel LM (1973) An examination of illegal aggression in intercollegiate hockey. In Williams I and Wankel LM (eds) *Proceedings of the fourth Canadian psychomotor learning and sport psychology symposium*, 531–42.

Weinberg R and Gould D (1995) *Foundations of sport and exercise psychology*. Champaign, Human Kinetics.

Weinberg RS and Weigand DA (1993) Goal-setting in sport and exercise: a reaction to Locke. *Journal of sport and exercise psychology* 15, 88–96.

Weinberg RS, Bruya LD, Jackson A and Garland H (1987) Goal difficulty and endurance performance: a challenge to the goal attainability assumption. *Journal of sport behaviour* 10, 82–93.

Weiner B (1974) *Achievement-motivation and attribution theory*. Morristown, General Learning Press.

Welford AT (1968) *Fundamentals of skill*. London, Methuen.

Wells CM, Collins D and Hale BD (1993) The self-efficacy–performance link in maximum strength performance. *Journal of sport sciences* 11, 167–75.

Williams JM (ed.) (1993) *Applied sport psychology, personal growth to peak performance*. Mountain View, Mayfield.

Yerkes RM and Dodson JD (1908) The relationship of strengh and stimulus to rapidity of habit formation. *Journal of comparative neurology and psychology* 18, 459–82.

Young K (1993) Violence, risk and liability in male sports culture. *Sociology of sport journal* 10, 373–96.

Zajonc RB (1965) Social facilitation. *Science* 149, 269–74.

Zaman H (1998) Are Muslim women excluded from the structures of sport and leisure? *Proceedings of the 1998 BPS annual conference* 6(2), 119.

Zuckerman M (1979) *Sensation seeking: beyond the optimum level of arousal*. Hillsdale, Lawrence Erlbaum Associates.

Index